Independence, Social, and Study Strategies for Young Adults with Autism Spectrum Disorder

of related interest

Student Resources:

**A Freshman Survival Guide for College Students
with Autism Spectrum Disorders**
The Stuff Nobody Tells You About!
Haley Moss
Foreword by Susan J. Moreno
ISBN 978 1 84905 984 8
eISBN 978 0 85700 922 7

Top Tips for Asperger Students
How to Get the Most Out of University and College
Rosemary Martin
ISBN 978 1 84905 140 8
eISBN 978 0 85700 341 6

**Succeeding as a Student in the STEM Fields
with an Invisible Disability**
A College Handbook for Science, Technology, Engineering,
and Math Students with Autism, ADD, Affective Disorders,
or Learning Difficulties and their Families
Christy Oslund
ISBN 978 1 84905 947 3
eISBN 978 0 85700 817 6

Professional Resources:

**Developing College Skills in Students
with Autism and Asperger's Syndrome**
Sarita Freedman
Foreword by Tony Attwood
ISBN 978 1 84310 917 4
eISBN 978 0 85700 292 1

**Helping Students with Autism Spectrum Disorder
Express their Thoughts and Knowledge in Writing**
Tips and Exercises for Developing Writing Skills
Elise Geither and Lisa Meeks
ISBN 978 1 84905 996 1
eISBN 978 0 85700 980 7

Supporting College and University Students with Invisible Disabilities
A Guide for Faculty and Staff Working with Students with Autism,
AD/HD, Language Processing Disorders, Anxiety, and Mental Illness
Christy Oslund
ISBN 978 1 84905 955 8
eISBN 978 0 85700 785 8

Independence, Social, and **Study Strategies** for Young Adults with Autism Spectrum Disorder

The BASICS College Curriculum

MICHELLE RIGLER,
AMY RUTHERFORD,
and EMILY QUINN

Jessica Kingsley *Publishers*
London and Philadelphia

Figure 3.1 on pages 65–7 (Sample Syllabus) is reproduced with kind permission of Dr. Ralph Covino. The Volcano illustration on page 118 is reproduced with kind permission of Elizabeth Aragon/Sweet ClipArt.

First published in 2015
by Jessica Kingsley Publishers
73 Collier Street
London N1 9BE, UK
and
400 Market Street, Suite 400
Philadelphia, PA 19106, USA

www.jkp.com

Library of Congress Cataloging in Publication Data
A CIP catalog record for this book is available from the Library of Congress

British Library Cataloguing in Publication Data
A CIP catalogue record for this book is available from the British Library

ISBN 978 1 84905 787 5
eISBN 978 1 78450 060 3

MIX
Paper from
responsible sources
FSC
www.fsc.org FSC® C013483

CONTENTS

ACKNOWLEDGMENTS

First, and foremost, we would like to thank our previous colleague and friend Leslie Harms. Leslie was the co-creator of the MoSAIC program and helped develop the first version of this curriculum. Her tireless effort to work outside her professional role helped make this curriculum and the program as a whole successful.

We wish to formally thank Dr. Nancy Badger for supporting the vision for a program that had no true boundaries. Although this is not something we had to do, she was able to recognize the need and fully supported our passion to do something that was completely "outside the box." You are a tremendous boss and mentor and your trust and willingness to let us pursue what is important to us means more than you can imagine.

We would also like to thank Dr. Jane Thierfeld-Brown for her leadership and advocacy in the field. You truly are the expert and mentor who helped form our program. Your visit to the University of Tennessee at Chattanooga in 2008 was more beneficial and had a greater impact than you can even imagine. Your book, *Students with Asperger Syndrome: A Guide for College Personnel*, is often referred to as our "bible" and it truly guided development and continues to guide our improvements.

Finally, our most sincere thanks go to the students in the MoSAIC program at the University of Tennessee at Chattanooga. You serve as a constant reminder that we don't know as much as we think we do, and you teach us daily.

INTRODUCTION

The opportunities and challenges presented in the college setting combine for both an exhilarating and demanding experience. Students are expected to master the skills that will guide them to academic success, but the college experience is much more than merely an academic endeavor. While we understand that students' primary goal during college is learning, our vision for this book is to help students with Autism Spectrum Disorder (ASD) develop strategies for learning not only in the academic arena, but the hidden social curriculum as well. By creating a system that emphasizes the skills necessary for transitioning to college, communicating with peers and instructors, studying, managing stress, and creating and maintaining relationships, we have tried to provide students on the spectrum with access to the "other" skills necessary for college success.

This guide is designed to outline the natural skills that neurotypical college students make use of every day to be successful college students. To have the opportunity to experience that same level of success, students with ASD will need to develop and practice those same sets of skills. The curriculum for this guide is formative in nature and has been adjusted over the years according to feedback given by students with ASD. Working with a group of college students with ASD has been a challenging and incredibly rewarding experience. We have used this direct experience to recognize what works and what needs improvement. Through research and first-hand experience as professionals working directly with students on the spectrum in a college environment, we have identified the areas in which many students with ASD struggle during their first year of college. These identified areas of potential growth have guided the focused development of this curriculum. The information and tools provided in this guide are fundamental to our vision of creating a program to help these students be successful, well-rounded, independent individuals.

Building on a foundation of consistently reinforced social skills, students who utilize the information in this text will be guided through various elements of the college experience with insight on the neurotypical perspective. In Chapter 1, a discussion of the transition to college is highlighted by life skills, self-advocacy, and understanding ASD. Chapter 2 presents a guide to getting organized academically, emphasizing time management, goal-setting, and prioritizing tasks. As students on the spectrum enter college, recognizing the need for and developing a system of organization in academics is one of the first steps students take to be academically successful. Then, in Chapter 3, the text is focused on communication skills needed for new college students. By guiding students through reviewing their syllabi, monitoring their progress, communicating with instructors, and understanding resources and how to ask for help, we seek to confirm the notion that being able to communicate effectively with professionals on a college campus can make a positive difference academically and socially. Chapter 4 guides students with ASD through medication management, daily preparation, personal care, and maintaining healthy living habits while they work to become organized in their personal life as newly independent college students. Just as it is important to know how to communicate with professionals on a college campus, students with ASD can use Chapter 5 to work on communicating in their personal lives by reviewing active communication, personal space, appropriate tone and volume when speaking, the reciprocal element of conversation, and topics which may be inappropriate for conversation on a college campus.

In Chapter 6, students will learn stress management techniques beginning with identifying stress and stress triggers, leading up to how to identify stress in relation to anger, and, finally, some coping strategies to deal with the stress of being a college student. Then, in Chapter 7, the text is focused on personal academic responsibility through a discussion of topics such as attendance, assignments, group work, study habits, and academic major and career exploration. Chapter 8 acts as a guide for students as they navigate their campus' social environment. Understanding social involvement through learning opportunities focused on a particular academic or personal interest, understanding marketability as a student, recognizing their college campus' community, and recognizing the need for and developing skills to ensure a solid social and academic balance are essential points of development for all college students, and particularly those with ASD. Finally, the text explores relationships in Chapter 9. Relationships can be confounding for students on the spectrum and, in the social world of college, understanding that, while there is no scientific formula for managing relationships, there are some standard social rules which can be the basis for students as they build a bridge between the world of ASD and that of neurotypicals.

This guide will present a set of tools throughout each chapter to help students with ASD fill their "social toolbox." The impact of ASD is highly individualized, so throughout this text, various methods will be used to convey the important messages. As with any student, the tools can be offered, but it is essentially up to the student to make use of them properly. Our primary method of reinforcing these concepts for the purposes of this guide will be to remind the students that in any situation and in any endeavor, it is always important to remember the BASICS.

The BASICS chart will be the conclusion to each chapter (see Table I.1 on page 12). Students will have a visual representation of the subject matter that is to be reflected upon in the same pattern for each chapter. While primarily providing a reflection on the understanding of the subject, the BASICS chart offers an opportunity for students to perform a confidential self-evaluation. Following the self-evaluation, students should be prepared to develop a set of short-term goals based on the areas of improvement identified through the BASICS chart. The goals should reflect the areas of improvement for: personal (hygiene, cleanliness, responsibility), academic (study, time management, reading, academic responsibility), and social (clubs, roommate relationships, feeling of belonging). Ideally, the BASICS charts will identify areas of strength and areas for potential growth for each section of the curriculum. As students move through the curriculum, this process will help them become better self-reflective, self-monitoring students. To see an example of how to implement the BASICS chart, see Appendix A.

This guide is intended to be a framework for working with students through the transition year into college. Professionals who work with students who have ASD can utilize the information presented in the text to facilitate discussions in a classroom setting, group setting, or individual meetings. Appendix B provides discussion points and questions that can be utilized by professionals as they see fit. The information presented is intended to be a starting point to be used with additional discussion, assignments, videos, etc. to best convey the information to specific student groups. Students using the text can take advantage of the reflection questions and worksheets to ensure a solid understanding of the topics presented. It is often the case that students benefit from consistent practice and consideration regarding new material, and we have designed the text to reflect this notion. In addition, the information in this guide can be used as individuals work to prepare themselves for the transition into and through higher education. Individuals can use this material and the guiding questions in Appendix B to move through this material independently or with support.

Students and professionals alike are encouraged to be creative with the material and to tailor it to their individual and circumstantial needs. While the material is written to provide knowledge and information about the college social and academic world for students with ASD, there is no limit to the ways in which the material can be utilized within a specific context, and this was intentional in our model. *Independence, Social, and Study Strategies for Young Adults with Autism Spectrum Disorder: The BASICS College Curriculum* is the result of a researched curriculum built upon significant feedback from those college students with ASD who gave us direction and purpose. We seek to provide our shared vision of opportunity and knowledge with students with ASD and those professionals who work with them during the exciting college experience.

All worksheets marked with the symbol ⬇ are available for download from the JKP website at www.jkp.com/catalogue/book/9781849057875/resources.

Table I.1 Back to BASICS Template

B	**Behavior** 1 2 3	Comments
A	**Academics** 1 2 3	Comments
S	**Self-care** 1 2 3	Comments
I	**Interaction** 1 2 3	Comments
C	**Community** 1 2 3	Comments
S	**Self-monitoring** 1 2 3	Comments

GOALS

Personal:

Academic:

Social:

Chapter 1

TRANSITION TO COLLEGE

The successful transition to college consists of a set of skills that need to be developed by every student making the journey.

TOOLS FOR SUCCESS

- Life skills development
    - Medical needs
    - Healthy eating habits
    - Keeping a clean self and living environment
    - Organization
    - Money management
- Self-advocacy
    - Self-advocating for living arrangements
    - Accommodations
    - Disclosing to professors
    - Peer self-advocacy
- Understanding Autism Spectrum Disorder
    - Impact triad
    - Theory of Mind
    - Central coherence theory
    - Executive functioning skills

INTRODUCTION

The transition to college is difficult for any student, but even more so for students with ASD. The social world of college may make students with ASD feel like they need a roadmap just to avoid the obstacles and navigate the path that comes more naturally for neurotypical students.

Throughout the development of this curriculum, feedback from students has been taken into account to direct where the focus of support is most needed. To develop skills in the area of transition, focus should be placed on the skills that are needed for independent living as a college student. These skills range from managing one's medication regimen to understanding the individual impact of ASD.

While the focus of this curriculum will not be based primarily on the negative aspects of ASD, it is vital for students transitioning into the post-secondary environment to have a strong understanding of the potential difficulties that could arise. Academically focused discussions around research-based theories can provide students with stronger understanding of ASD and help them to identify potential roadblocks before they become a detour to their path of success.

For independent students, it is increasingly more important to become strong self-advocates. Developing an understanding of ASD and the impact this group of disabilities can have on an individual student can help drive those conversations. By truly understanding the impact, students can speak to their own needs with more confidence.

LESSON 1: LIFE SKILLS DEVELOPMENT

A part of transition to college is learning how to do all the tasks that parents have typically done for their children. Students come to college with the expectation that they will now need to monitor their eating habits, keep their living environment clean, clean their own laundry, develop and maintain their own schedule, etc. Many students with ASD have difficulties with the most primary of behaviors like setting alarms and getting themselves up for classes.

To begin this process of identifying strength areas and areas of development, identify the independent skills you do yourself or are done by others. Please complete this checklist independently and honestly. This information will help develop a baseline of skills so you can be best supported during your time of transition.

What are some additional areas that you would like to work on this year to become a more independent adult?

_____

_____

_____

_____

_____

_____

_____

_____

_____

_____

_____

_____

INDEPENDENT LIFE SKILLS DEVELOPMENT

Circle the word that most closely matches your level of skill regarding the following list of independent life skills.

Set alarms	Independent	With help	Dependent
Wake up alone	Independent	With help	Dependent
Manage hygiene	Independent	With help	Dependent
Set daily schedule	Independent	With help	Dependent
Manage daily schedule	Independent	With help	Dependent
Monitor eating habits	Independent	With help	Dependent
Cook meals	Independent	With help	Dependent
Keep my room clean	Independent	With help	Dependent
Do laundry	Independent	With help	Dependent
Transportation	Independent	With help	Dependent
Shopping	Independent	With help	Dependent
Monitor medication	Independent	With help	Dependent
Budgeting	Independent	With help	Dependent
Check emails	Independent	With help	Dependent
Communicate needs	Independent	With help	Dependent
Conflict resolution	Independent	With help	Dependent
Asking for help	Independent	With help	Dependent

MEDICAL NEEDS

A primary area of needed skills for students is the area of medical/health management. It is vital for you to have an understanding of when to seek medical attention, how to process insurance paperwork, who to contact in case of an emergency, and how to manage your medication regimen.

It is imperative for you to have vital medical information prior to the time it is needed. This includes things such as insurance information, family physician, medication dosages, diagnosis, etc. If you have this information prior to requiring medical attention, you will not be trying to find the answers to these questions during a time of medical need.

Too often, students come to college with little understanding of the impact of their medication. This means they do not understand the importance of the medication and so may forget to take prescriptions as directed. This could have a potentially negative effect on physical health, mental health, and academic standing. It is best for you to know why you take medication and what could happen if you choose to stop taking it. In addition, students often see the transition to college as a time to "do things on their own" without the assistance of medication. This trend is often the cause of students failing during the initial transition to college. During this time, medication is more important than ever. It is better to start college taking medication regularly, and then work with the prescribing professional to stop taking the medication if that is the choice. The following form is provided for you to complete, so you will have this information to hand when you need it.

EMERGENCY CONTACT AND MEDICAL INFORMATION

Full Name: _____ Date of Birth: _____

Phone Number: _____

PRIMARY EMERGENCY CONTACT

Name: _____

Relationship: _____

Home/Cell Phone Number: _____

Work Phone Number: _____

SECONDARY EMERGENCY CONTACT

Name: _____

Relationship: _____

Home/Cell Phone Number: _____

Work Phone Number: _____

MEDICAL INFORMATION

Primary Physician Name: _____ Phone: _____

Insurance Company: _____ Phone: _____

Policy Number: _____

Health considerations: _____

_____

_____

_____

_____

_____

_____

Allergies and Treatment: _____

_____

_____

_____

_____

_____

MEDICATION INFORMATION

Prescription Medication: _____

Dosage: _____ Frequency: _____

Purpose: _____

Helpful effects: _____

Potential harmful effects: _____

Prescription Medication: _____

Dosage: _____ Frequency: _____

Purpose: _____

Helpful effects: _____

Potential harmful effects: _____

Prescription Medication: _____

Dosage: _____   Frequency: _____

Purpose: _____

Helpful effects: _____

Potential harmful effects: _____

Prescription Medication: _____

Dosage: _____   Frequency: _____

Purpose: _____

Helpful effects: _____

Potential harmful effects: _____

Over-the-counter Medication: _____

_____

_____

What would be the effect if you stopped taking your medication?

_____

_____

_____

_____

_____

Are there any medications you would like to stop taking? Why?

_____

_____

_____

_____

HEALTHY EATING HABITS

For a student with ASD moving into independence in the college environment, one area that may be of particular difficulty is the specific dietary needs that may exist. Although many college campuses have a great variety of food available, the food served at school will not be what you are used to at home. The best approach to developing flexibility in diet is to determine what a dietary preference is, as opposed to a dietary restriction. For example, if you are lactose intolerant, you have a dietary restriction which means you can not consume foods with dairy. If you prefer only peanut butter and jelly sandwiches for lunch, this is a dietary preference.

In most college settings, there are a variety of food plans to choose from, but there will be a need for some flexibility on the part of students. Although the food will not be what you are used to, this is a great time to try new food options. A good way to develop control over eating habits is to keep a food diary. In this diary, you should note true dietary needs/restrictions, dietary preferences, texture intolerances, and meal times, and allow some space to document new food choices and reflections about those choices.

During this time, it is possible to gain or lose weight due to the change in eating habits. You should be very aware of your own food intake and monitor the effects the new food choices are having on your body. Changing eating habits does not need to equate to gaining the "freshman 15" (the 15 pounds that students typically gain in their first year at college/university) or becoming physically ill, but it is your responsibility to monitor your own eating habits and make changes as needed.

You can complete the following example of a Food Diary, or create your own.

FOOD DIARY

Dietary allergies: _____

_____

_____

Dietary restrictions: _____

_____

_____

Dietary preferences: _____

_____

_____

Texture intolerances: _____

_____

_____

Meal time preferences:

    Breakfast _____   Lunch _____   Dinner _____

New food choices and reflections:

_____

_____

_____

_____

KEEPING A CLEAN SELF AND LIVING ENVIRONMENT

Students with ASD can often be at the polar opposites of hygiene and cleanliness. You may be hyper-focused on a clean living environment or it may be one of the least important topics to focus on for you. Whether you are living on campus or commuting for classes, you will be sharing close spaces with hundreds of other students. Cleanliness and flexibility with others' habits are vital features of helping you reach a sense of belonging within your campus culture.

Because many students with ASD do not focus their primary attention on personal hygiene and cleanliness in their living environment, it is important to build these items into a set organizational system. Developing a daily and weekly planning system will help you build in these necessary, but often overlooked, activities of independent living.

Determining the baseline for these skills is important in order to know the appropriate level of support needed to help you further develop these skills.

CLEANLINESS SELF-PERCEPTION

Answer the following questions to create a baseline of skills to develop a support plan.

1. How often do you brush your teeth, shower, wash hair, etc.?

    _____

    _____

2. Do you know how to do laundry?

    _____

3. How many times a week do you clean your clothes?

    _____

4. How often should you clean your dishes/kitchen?

    _____

5. How often should you clean your room?

    _____

6. How do you share responsibility with roommates to keep common areas clean?

    _____

    _____

7. What are your personal concerns about this area?

    _____

    _____

    _____

CLEANLINESS CHECKLIST

Use the following checklist to keep track of your hygiene.

☐ Brush your teeth twice a day.

☐ Shower daily.

☐ Wear deodorant daily.

☐ Clean your dishes after every use.

☐ Do your laundry every weekend.

☐ Clean your room every weekend.

☐ Clean your bathroom every other week.

☐ Develop a shared living agreement with roommates each semester.

ORGANIZATION

Full-time college students have similar requirements to a person working a full-time job. If you are a student carrying 12 credit hours, you should expect to work at least 40 hours each week on school assignments and studying. This requirement also includes managing expectations from several different directions, such as expectations from professors, peers, parents, coaches, advisors, etc. Without a consistent organizational system, you could forget vital appointments or assignments. Many times, students with ASD claim to be able to keep things organized in their heads without the aid of an organizational system, but as you transition to college, your existing system will be challenged.

To be a successful college student, you will need to create an organizational system that begins with a wide view and narrows to a more detailed view. The wide view of organization will include a semester calendar that reflects the major assignments and tests for each class. Then you can narrow that view into a weekly calendar that focuses on the individual assignments and study requirements for the week. Finally, you can outline daily requirements that include hygiene requirements, class meeting times, study group meetings, meals, and personal time.

People with ASD tend to be specific-to-general thinkers. This means that you may pay close attention to details, define how details relate to each other, categorize and sub-categorize these details, and then put them all together to create the larger picture. This way of thinking is beneficial in many ways, but it makes the process of creating an organizational system difficult. You should work with someone to create a system and follow it consistently to create the habit of being an organized student.

WHAT IS YOUR CURRENT ORGANIZATIONAL SYSTEM?

Semester

_____

_____

Weekly

_____

_____

Daily

_____

_____

What works for you?

_____

_____

_____

MONEY MANAGEMENT

Prior to college, the responsibility to manage money is usually with parents. As you enter college, this responsibility shifts to you, and you must create and adhere to a budget system. Individuals on the spectrum will especially benefit from developing a budget system during their transition to independent living. It is important for you to find an effective method for managing money that works with your preference. Some helpful tools for creating and managing money include online budget templates, phone apps, a cash envelope system, or the mobile or online banking option for your specific bank.

Consult with your parents or life coach, if you have one, to determine strategies for your individual financial obligations. (A life coach is a person to consult and work with consistently to help set up the systems to manage all aspects of life, including executive functioning skills, organizational strategies, time management techniques, money management, and academic fluency.) The common phrase "living within your means" suggests limiting your impulsive spending to stay within your budgeted allowance. Monitor your spending with regard to the logical and effective distribution of your money. This will enable you to save for unforeseen emergencies and to understand when spending on leisure items or activities is appropriate. Budgeting can be a very rewarding skill to develop during college as you begin to plan for your future.

One special point you should take note of is the ability to have many things money-related available online. While it is a great idea to make use of online banking options so you have access to your balance at all times, you should also be very careful about putting your debit or credit card information online for purchases. This could open you up to having multiple charges against your bank account when your intention was only one charge.

LESSON 2: SELF-ADVOCACY

Neurotypical college students often have difficulties talking about the things they may need from peers, roommates, and professors. This difficulty is amplified for college students with ASD. Discussing personal challenges can be difficult and embarrassing for people, but if you are not able to talk about your needs, those needs may go unmet.

Some things you may need to be prepared for as a student with ASD are voicing personal space needs in roommate agreements, discussing personal plans with peers, and advocating for your academic accommodations with professors, and, possibly, the ability to appropriately disclose your ASD diagnosis. This is a scary thing to do, but practicing these skills will make them more manageable.

Some beneficial ways to practice these skills are creating contracts prior to a meeting, developing a checklist of needs prior to a meeting, writing a script, and practicing the conversation with someone who understands the difficulties faced by students with ASD. Although telling someone about a disability is not something people like to do, it is important in the case of disclosing ASD. As a student with ASD, you typically do not have an apparent physical disability that people notice daily. The impact is invisible, but often carries a greater impression because the effect tends to be placed primarily in the social capacity of the person. College itself is a very social environment and college students tend to live through the established social rules of the college campus. This is the area that is a consistent struggle for students with ASD. By talking openly about the impact of ASD, you may become an empowered self-advocate.

SELF-ADVOCATING FOR LIVING ARRANGEMENTS

As you begin your next stage of life, many of you will choose to live on campus in the residence halls. Living with roommates can be an experience that encourages tremendous growth, but can also be very difficult to manage. Developing a roommate contract in the beginning can help alleviate the stressors that could develop later in the semester. When you work with your roommates to develop your living agreement, be sure to be open and honest about what you will need in your living environment while also respecting what the needs of your roommates may be.

Some areas to consider in developing your roommate contract could include things such as quiet times in the main living space, labeling and asking permission to use personal items, the expected level of cleanliness in the common areas, times for visitors, and the temperature of the living area. These may not be the only things addressed in a roommate contract, but this will give you an idea of things that can be addressed prior to them becoming an issue in your living space.

The development of a roommate contract alone will not solve all issues that may come up between roommates. At some point, you may need to address conflict with roommates not following the contract. Use the following contract and scripts as examples for how these periods of conflict can be prevented. You can download and print out a copy of the following roommate agreement.

ROOMMATE CONTRACT

CLEANING THE SHARED LIVING SPACE

☐ We will have a designated space for everything.

☐ We will keep the space clean but not perfect.

☐ We plan to clean up after ourselves.

☐ We are OK with leaving things lying around.

We will share cleaning responsibilities in the following way:

_____

_____

_____

STUDY TIME

We plan to study during the hours of _____ to _____.

During study hours it is OK to:

   Have complete silence Play music Watch TV Talk

For study groups it is OK to:

   Study in the room Go to a public space

TEMPERATURE OF ROOM

We agree to keep the temperature of the room at _____ and agree to consult with each other before changing the temperature.

SOCIALIZING IN THE ROOM

It is OK to socialize in the common area of the room from the hours of _____ to _____.
There will be quiet times in the common areas between the times of _____ to _____.

SLEEPING BEHAVIORS

The following behaviors are unacceptable while roommates are sleeping:

_____

_____

_____

_____

_____

_____

WE AGREE TO SHARE THE FOLLOWING

TV   Stereo   Computer   Video Games   Appliances   Dishes   Food

Notes: _____

_____

_____

_____

_____

_____

_____

COMMUNICATION

If there is a disagreement between us, we agree that:

☐ We will discuss the issue directly with the person.

☐ We will not talk behind roommates' backs.

☐ We will go directly to the resident advisor.

☐ We will not ignore the problem hoping it goes away.

SPECIFIC NEEDS NOT ADDRESSED IN THIS CONTRACT

_____

_____

_____

_____

By signing this, we enter into this official agreement with all roommates

Name: _____

Signature: _____

ID: _____**Bed space:** _____

Date: _____

Residence Life Staff: _____ **Date:** _____

ROOMMATE SCRIPT

EXAMPLE

"When we moved in, we agreed in the roommate contract that from 12AM to 7AM would be quiet times in the room, but this week you have been playing your music loudly at 2AM. This has made it very difficult for me to sleep and be ready for my 8AM class. Can you please turn your music down during this time?"

SCENARIO

Your roommate is using your dishes and leaving them dirty in the sink. This has happened three times in the last week. Write a script for how you can address this with the roommate.

_____

_____

_____

_____

_____

_____

_____

_____

_____

_____

_____

_____

_____

_____

_____

_____

_____

_____

_____

ACCOMMODATIONS

Sometimes it is important to reach out to services offered on your campus to help you manage your in-class accommodations. These support services are housed differently from campus to campus but you should be aware that these services are available. If you are in need of academic accommodations on your campus it is important to learn how this process works. The following is an example of what an accommodation request form might look like.

ACCOMMODATION REQUEST FORM

THIS FORM CERTIFIES THAT THE FOLLOWING STUDENT HAS PRESENTED THE REQUIRED DOCUMENTATION TO SUPPORT A DISABILITY AS DEFINED BY THE AMERICANS WITH DISABILITIES ACT.

The information contained in this document is CONFIDENTIAL and should not be disclosed to a third party without the expressed permission of the student (see A.D.A. Title 1 at 42 USC ss12112(d)(3) & (4);29 cfr ss 1630.14-1630.16). Any questions should be referred to the Office of Disability Service.

Student name: _____ **ID:** _____

TO EQUALIZE THIS STUDENT'S CHANCES FOR ACADEMIC SUCCESS, THE FOLLOWING ACCOMMODATIONS ARE NECESSARY:

Extended time on all tests in all subjects: time-and-a-half should be given

Testing in a distraction-reduced environment

Use of tape recorder in classroom

Priority registration

Lab partner for assistance

Use of a calculator during tests

Student Signature: _____ **Date:** _____

Staff signature: _____ **Date:** _____

DISCLOSING TO PROFESSORS

Understanding your college's process for requesting accommodations is important, but knowing how to articulate your specific needs regarding your accommodations to your professors is just as important. Use the professor script which fwollows to help prompt you on how to formulate your communication. Note that you have a choice of whether or not you disclose the reason for your accommodations.

PROFESSOR SCRIPT

EXAMPLES

NON-DISCLOSURE OF ASD

"Hi, Professor _____, my name is _____. I am a student registered with the Disability Resource Center and I have an accommodation request letter to give you. My accommodations are pretty easy to manage and I am committed to working hard in your class. If you have any questions about these accommodations, please just let me know."

DISCLOSURE OF ASD

"Hi, Professor _____, my name is _____. I am a student registered with the Disability Resource Center. I am also a student with an Autism Spectrum Disorder (*or you could be more specific and say, with Autism, or with Asperger's syndrome*). I know that people are sometimes confused about what autism is and I would be happy to tell you how it affects me if you would like to know. Just let me know if you have any questions about my particular qualities as a student."

SCENARIO

If a request for accommodations has been made appropriately, the professor is required to engage in an interactive conversation with the disability service provider and the student to find reasonable accommodation that will not change the fundamental requirements of the class. After you disclose your information to your professor, he says it is too much work to provide you with accommodations in his class. He then asks you to switch to another section. His section fits in very well with your schedule and you already know some people in the class so you do not want to switch. Write a script for how you would address this with the professor.

_____

_____

_____

_____

_____

_____

_____

_____

_____

_____

_____

PEER SELF-ADVOCACY

Not all neurotypical college students will approach students with ASD with kindness. Some peers will lack patience, be rude, or even bully you. Sometimes, neurotypical college students will use sarcasm and mixed messages, which may confuse you. It is important to recognize these things and develop a strategy for how to manage situations as they arise.

In the new college culture, you will be interacting with a wide variety of students from different geographic locations, from different cultures, from different backgrounds, and with a variety of degrees of understanding about ASD. As a self-advocate, it is your responsibility to question the intentions of your peers and address any difficulty as it arises.

Although it may be difficult to recognize the true intentions of people, it is helpful to discuss and reflect on some confusing social interactions with a trusted person. Analyze the interaction and share your perception with someone you trust who can verify or challenge your view of the interaction. It is also important to have some social scripts prepared to address any immediate situations. Practicing scripts and role-play will make these situations less stressful.

Scripts can be used in many ways. They can be written scripts that you prepare ahead of time and follow during conversations, or they can be developed and practiced prior to some common social interactions, like small talk. However you choose to use the script method, know that they can be helpful in preparing for and managing difficult conversations.

PEER SCRIPT

SCENARIO

You have got to know one of your roommates fairly well and s/he begins to ask questions about why you do some of the things you do. In particular, your roommate asks you why you interrupt people all the time when they are talking. How could you respond to this?

EXAMPLE

"I'm sorry that I interrupt. Because I have Asperger's (*or ASD, Autism, as appropriate*) sometimes I don't understand the social cues of communication but I am working on it. If I start to interrupt when other people are here, can you give me a sign that I am doing that and it will help me know when to talk and when to stop."

SCENARIO

While working on a class project in a group, a group member tells you that you are clearly the smartest person in the group and the rest of them have a big party to go to this weekend. At this point, the group member says that you should just go ahead and do the project and send it to the group through email so they can add their suggestions. Develop your own script for this situation.

_____

_____

_____

_____

_____

_____

_____

_____

_____

_____

_____

_____

_____

_____

_____

_____

LESSON 3: UNDERSTANDING AUTISM SPECTRUM DISORDER

Autism Spectrum Disorders are a confusing and often misunderstood group of diagnoses. Students with ASD may not even have a true understanding of the individual impact of ASD. Moving into the new social structure of a college environment gives students the opportunity to become the experts on their disability.

While growing up, you may possibly have heard of the diagnoses of Attention Deficit Disorder (ADD), Bi-Polar Disorder, and Obsessive Compulsive Disorder (OCD) all in reference to yourself, but perhaps none of them quite fitted. At some point, the qualified professionals settled on a diagnosis of ASD. While the adults and professionals understand what this means, you may have been left confused. So, during this transition into adulthood, it is vital to understand the global and individual impact of ASD. To be able to effectively advocate for your needs, you must understand your difficulties and strengths, and be able to identify your specific needs.

Many psychological theories exist that attempt to identify the impact of ASD. In this section, the Impact Triad is introduced and revisited frequently throughout this curriculum. In addition, the three major psychological theories that are most frequently combined to examine ASD's global impact are Theory of Mind, Central Coherence Theory, and Executive Functioning Skills.

IMPACT TRIAD

ASD tends to affect people in a combination of three different areas. These areas include social/emotional issues, flexibility of thought, and communication (Attwood 2006). A person with ASD may be affected in all three areas equally or only one area. It depends on the personal impact and the strategies you have developed over time. Each area is significant in a social culture such as a college campus and can significantly affect the feeling of belonging and academic success.

SOCIAL/EMOTIONAL ISSUES

This portion of the Impact Triad affects how you manage relationships with peers, roommates, girlfriends/boyfriends, parents, and professors. The impact in this area may cause confusion when determining the nature of a relationship, managing healthy relationships, understanding how to approach different people in different ways, and how to advocate for yourself in relationships. This area also contributes to the lack of understanding of social rules and why they exist. Finally, the impact in this area can be the root of anxiety during unstructured time. With much more free time than you are used to, like many college students with ASD, you may struggle during your transition to college. When occupying free time with social activities seems natural for your neurotypical peers, the confusion that exists when you approach free time differently may lead to a feeling of isolation if this area is not supported.

FLEXIBILITY OF THOUGHT

This portion of the Impact Triad deals with the ability to see other people's perspectives, difficulty with schedule changes, generalizing information, and recognizing the contributions of others. In a college setting, this area of development is vital due to the inclusive nature of the culture. As a college student, you will be expected to think critically and participate in discussions with peers and professors. This can be a challenge because thinking critically involves recognizing the perspective of others, analyzing that perspective, and shifting personal perspectives as needed. This shift is where you, as a student with ASD, can get caught. In addition, many college courses require group projects for a major portion of the grade for the course. This is an area where you can stumble as well, but for two very distinct reasons. You could either become nervous about the social interaction of the group and disengage from the work that needs to be completed, or you could become the workhorse for the group and not recognize that you are doing more of the work than the other members. Finally, generalizing information from lectures is the key to academic success. Students in college are not just expected to memorize and recite information. They are expected to process information, think critically about that information, and be able to synthesize that information to be used in a more general sense. Without support helping you and other students with ASD generalize the information, you could face a difficult challenge in managing all the information presented in each class. Without attaching meaning, information may seem irrelevant to you.

COMMUNICATION

The communication portion of the Impact Triad addresses both verbal and non-verbal communication. Students with ASD typically have a difficult time with social language that involves nuance, sarcasm, multiple meanings, etc. This area of impact is especially notable in the college culture due to the language play that takes place constantly between peers. In a conversation with college students, phrases can have any number of meanings depending on the context of the conversation. As a student with ASD, you may hear phrases like "my phone is blowing up" or "I'm making it rain" and have no reference point for what the speaker is intending. This may make you feel like an outsider in conversations. In addition, you may have a difficult time recognizing the body language of a person with whom you are interacting. For instance, if a peer is looking away from the speaker and checking the time, a neurotypical college student would recognize that either that person is in a hurry to leave, or is no longer interested in the conversation. Either way, they would recognize that the other person is done with the conversation. This kind of non-verbal cue is something that may be difficult for you to recognize. Being able to navigate conversations and interactions with peers is what will help you feel like you belong in the college community. With the ability to question interactions and responses with someone who is trusted, you can manage this difficult process.

What are your initial thoughts about each of the three areas of the Impact Triad? Do you feel that these areas are accurate?

_____

_____

_____

_____

_____

_____

_____

_____

_____

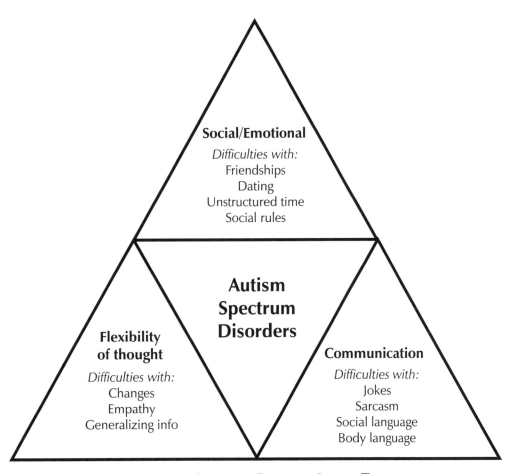

FIGURE 1.1 AUTISM SPECTRUM DISORDER IMPACT TRIAD

How do each of these areas impact you? Write your answers on the blank Triad below.

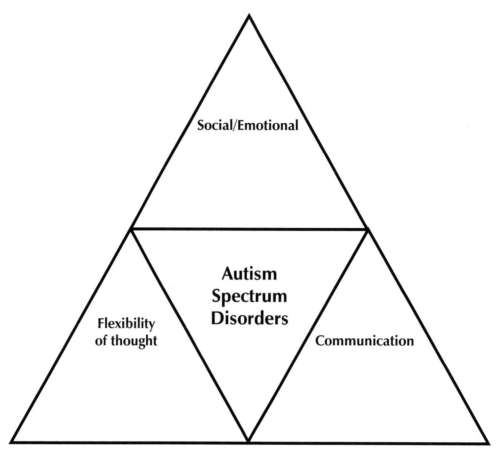

FIGURE 1.2 AUTISM SPECTRUM DISORDER IMPACT TRIAD

THEORY OF MIND

Simply stated, Theory of Mind is the capacity to understand other people's mental states as the reason for behavior (Attwood 2006; Baron-Cohen, Leslie and Frith, 1985). A major component of this theory is the ability to recognize that others have different perspectives. When a person imagines others' feelings, intentions, hopes and desires, they are able to predict others' behavior based on those mental states. This ability to predict behavior makes social interactions much more manageable and natural. In neurotypical college students this ability allows them to try to read each other by postures, gestures, or expressions, but they also know that people are trying to read them, so they try to hide their true feelings by using masking behaviors. This makes the social structure even more difficult to navigate for students with ASD.

Although many people see this as an innate skill set that you either have or you do not, we choose to see this as a skill set that can be developed. Much like an ethnographic researcher studying other cultures, the development of this skill should be based on cultural observations. As a student with ASD, you may typically see details instead of the larger picture, so taking the approach of an ethnographic researcher will allow you to use this detail-oriented strength to observe and discuss the postures, gestures, and expressions of your same-aged peers in this new college culture. By observing a social situation and opening conversations about the noted details, you can build these skills.

CENTRAL COHERENCE THEORY

Central coherence can be described as being the conductor of your life. Much like a conductor of an orchestra brings in sounds, timing, and feeling from many different parts into one cohesive and meaningful piece of music, people must be able to bring all the pieces of their lives together to form a complete picture of important elements. Central coherence is essentially the ability to be able to pull information from all areas to develop a higher meaning (Frith 2003; Frith and Hill 2003). A neurotypical college student may look at acres of trees and see a forest; a student with ASD may look at that same group of trees and see individual trees with individual traits.

Like other students with ASD, you may tend to excel in the areas that require significant focus on the details of a topic, but sequencing those details and arranging them into a meaningful bigger picture may be difficult. To help build these skills, you may relate putting pieces of information together to putting together a jigsaw puzzle. Without the pieces, the puzzle will never come together but also, without a picture of what the puzzle is supposed to look like, there is no direction for progress. Creating a concrete puzzle of what your future will look like, then separating the larger picture into smaller pieces labeled with what is required to be successful will help make sense of this concept. Labeling the back of each puzzle piece with things that could include "go to class," "study," "stay organized," "talk with professors," "ask questions," etc. could help you see that the skills required to be successful include more than being smart or good at math.

EXECUTIVE FUNCTIONING SKILLS

Executive functioning skills are a set of mental processes that help us connect our past experiences with things required to take action in a present situation. They allow people to access information from previous experiences, assess the outcomes of those experiences, develop a set of outcomes based on those experiences, and apply and implement the solutions to a set of present problems (Ozonoff, Dawson, and McPartland 2002). Neurotypical college students have developed these higher-level thinking skills to help them prioritize, multi-task, and guide themselves to be successful in college. For students with ASD, this may not come as naturally.

For you, as a student with ASD, this could mean difficulties with prioritizing tasks, setting a schedule, staying organized, self-motivation, managing impulsivity, and what we refer to as "getting stuck." "Getting stuck" in this sense refers to what happens when you become anxious about changes and cannot move forward due to the inflexibility inherent in this new environment. Executive functioning skills impact areas of life that include more than academics. Difficulties with executive functioning skills could also impact budgeting, relationships, health, and work life. Without a strong skill set and the ability to take advantage of supports in place to help you, you may feel buried by hundreds of small tasks.

As with any skill set, this can be improved with practice. You will need to be willing to try new things to discover a system that works for you. Things such as prioritized "To Do" lists, daily and weekly schedules, visual reminders, and creating steps to complete large projects will be necessary added steps to support academic success in a college environment.

Identify the skills needed in each of these areas on the figure below.

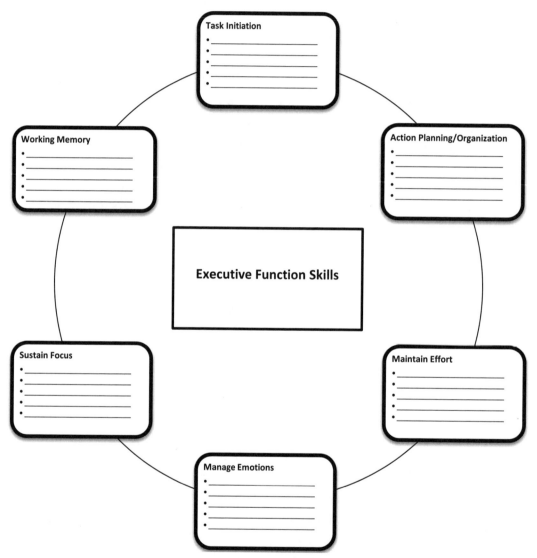

FIGURE 1.3 EXECUTIVE FUNCTION SKILLS

Identify the areas of strength and weakness for yourself:

_____

_____

_____

_____

_____

_____

_____

_____

_____

_____

Goals for improvement for the next month:

_____

_____

_____

_____

_____

_____

_____

_____

_____

_____

_____

_____

_____

_____

_____

THE BASICS

Throughout each chapter of this book you will be asked to revisit this chart and rate yourself on this important set of principles and how they are guiding the growth in the area of study for the chapter. Throughout transition and the years spent in college, it is vital to always focus on the BASICS. This focused set of principles will be helpful for students with ASD to become responsible, self-aware college students.

B	Behavior	Are you aware of how you come across to others? Do you understand the body language of your peers? How are you managing your frustrations? What are your reactions to suggestions? Have you identified some of your challenges?
A	Academics	Are you attending all your classes? Are you applying organizational strategies? Are you using your support team? Are you keeping up with everything? Are you completing study hours?
S	Self-care	Are you getting enough sleep? Are you eating healthily? Are you keeping yourself clean? Are you keeping your space clean? Are you managing your stress level?
I	Interaction	Are you checking in with your support team? Are you interacting with your peers well? Are you actively engaged in classes? Are you meeting your obligations? Are you checking your email/blackboard daily?
C	Community	Do you feel like you belong? Are you asking for help when needed? Have you met anyone new? Do you know the names of any classmates? Are you involved in anything socially?
S	Self-monitoring	Are you managing your time? Are you accepting critical feedback? Are you managing your frustration level? Are you willing to see the perspectives of others? Are you advocating for yourself?

BACK TO BASICS: RATE YOURSELF

Following your self-evaluation you should spend time developing short-term goals surrounding your areas of growth. The ratings will change frequently as they are based on situations and personal growth. Rate yourself with 1 being low and 3 being high. Be honest as you rate your growth in each area.

B	**Behavior** 1 2 3	**Comments**
A	**Academics** 1 2 3	**Comments**
S	**Self-care** 1 2 3	**Comments**
I	**Interaction** 1 2 3	**Comments**
C	**Community** 1 2 3	**Comments**
S	**Self-monitoring** 1 2 3	**Comments**

GOALS

Personal:

Academic:

Social:

Chapter 2

ORGANIZATION IN ACADEMICS

Getting organized early is a key to a smooth semester. Beginning the semester with a solid organization system and using that system consistently throughout the entire semester can be the difference between a semester of playing catch-up and a semester of academic success.

TOOLS FOR SUCCESS

- Planning systems
  ○ Types of planners
  ○ Using technology to plan
- Managing time and assignments
- Setting goals

INTRODUCTION

Creating an organization system is a vital strategy for managing college life. Let's be honest—college is more than just academics. College is a time for personal growth and development and this goes beyond the obvious goal of academic excellence. Students are expected to manage their academic commitments in addition to an array of social opportunities, part-time jobs, and personal time. During mid-term and final exams, for example, students must prioritize their social, personal, and academic responsibilities in order to maintain or increase their study time to perform well during their exams. Using a planning system is fundamental to the organization process. Students who master the use of their individual planning system are prepared to manage their time for assignments and exams, classroom attendance, social events, and personal relaxation.

Setting up a planning system, managing time, and setting goals are essential skills leading to success at college.

Students with ASD can have difficulties in the area of executive functioning, which is essentially the skill set needed to maintain an organized approach in college. Because the successful management of time and priorities is so important, it is imperative that students with ASD develop a consistent system of organization (Wolf, Brown, and Bork 2009) that they will commit to and use effectively during their time in college.

LESSON 1: PLANNING SYSTEMS

Whether it is a two-year detailed by-the-hour schedule book, or a simple weekly calendar folded up in your pocket, planning during college is the first step to effective organization and time management. There are many methods for planning and scheduling, and it is important to recognize which ones can help you be as consistent as possible. Some recommended methods include a semester, weekly, or daily schedule sheet, color-block scheduling, computer-aided planning, smart phones used for planning, and visual reminders and notifications.

A solid planning system will begin with the big picture in mind, and then narrow to a moderate level of detail, followed by the most detailed planner that looks at the daily requirements. In addition, a desk or wall calendar allows you to be visually reminded of the assignments, exams, appointments, and events weeks in advance. Using color to identify time blocks offers a visual representation of your time each day. Setting visual reminders can encourage students with ASD to avoid hyper-focusing so they can use their time more effectively.

Both neurotypical college students and college students with ASD have affection for technology. Electronic devices such as computers, tablets, and smart phones allow you to plan using options other than a pen and a planner. Whatever you decide to use to plan your time, it is important that you understand how college life demands more than remembering your homework for the next day.

TYPES OF PLANNERS

Semester

Students with ASD often have a very difficult time seeing the big picture of a semester of work. To combat this, it is vital for you to begin the semester in a very organized and structured way. You should begin this process before classes even begin.

Most college campuses use online course management programs where professors can post the syllabi for their class prior to the semester beginning. You can begin your semesters by developing a semester planning system in which the full four months of course requirements can be seen easily. This can be done through wall calendars, desk calendars, whiteboard calendars, or quarterly-based paper planners.

Once you decide which system works best for you, print out the syllabus for each course and begin the process of documenting the requirements. For each course, you should identify the due dates of major assignments, presentations, and exams. You should then transfer each of these dates onto their semester planner system to serve as a visual reminder for what is coming up. Other important things to add to the semester planners are doctors appointments that can't be missed, vacations, or any other reason classes would be missed.

This step may take a time commitment at the beginning of each semester, but it is likely to give you the added support needed to develop and maintain an organized semester.

Sun	Mon	Tue	Wed	Thu	Fri	Sat
				1	2	3
4	5	6	7	8	9	10
11	12	13	14	15 Math Exam	16	17
18	19 Dr. appt.	20	21	22	23	24
25	26 Hist. Exam	27	28	29	30	31
January						

Sun	Mon	Tue	Wed	Thu	Fri	Sat
1	2	3	4	5	6 Engl. Paper	7
8	9	10	11	12	13	14
15	16 Hist. Exam	17 Chem. Exam	18 Engl. Exam	19 Math Exam	20	21
22	23 Dr. appt.	24	25	26	27	28
February						

Sun	Mon	Tue	Wed	Thu	Fri	Sat
1	2	3	4	5	6	7
8	9 Dr. appt.	10	11	12	13	14
15	16 spring break	17 spring break	18 spring break	19 spring break	20 spring break	21
22	23	24	25 Math Exam	26	27	28
29	30 Hist. Exam	31 Engl. Present				
March						

Sun	Mon	Tue	Wed	Thu	Fri	Sat
			1	2	3	4
5	6	7 Chem. Exam	8	9	10 Math Exam	11
12	13 Dr. appt.	14	15	16	17	18
19	20	21 Engl. Paper	22 Math final	23 Hist. final	23 Che4. final	25 Move out
26	27	28	29	30		
April						

FIGURE 2.1 SEMESTER PLANNER EXAMPLE

WEEKLY

Once you have started the semester in an organized way, it is imperative that you continue this pattern of organization. Once the semester plan has been established, it will be easier to plan for which pieces of assignments need to be completed throughout each week. By checking the visual reminders for each month, you can transfer not only test dates and assignment due dates, but also course meeting times and times to study. This can help dictate how you should manage your free time.

Students with ASD can get overwhelmed by the large-scale projects for classes that are due months down the line. Using this weekly planning system will help you manage that workload. By revisiting the visual calendar for the semester, you can identify the due dates for major projects. With the help of a support team, you can then break those projects down into manageable chunks with individual due dates. You can then responsibly monitor your own progress throughout the semester to ensure that the major projects are completed on time. In addition, students with ASD can schedule hygiene as a reminder and study time in the weekly planner so they do not get hyper-focused on one subject or get immersed in special interest topics at the expense of studying.

Table 2.1 Weekly Planner Example

	Sun	Mon	Tues	Wed	Thurs	Fri	Sat
7AM		Breakfast & Brush	Breakfast & Brush	Breakfast & Brush	Breakfast & Brush	Breakfast & Brush	
8AM		English	Shower	English	Shower	English	
9AM	Shower						
10AM		DRC	Math	Chem. Lab	Math	DRC	Clean Room
11AM	Study		Math	Chem. Lab	Math		Clean Room
12PM		Lunch	Lunch	Lunch	Lunch	Lunch	
1PM	Lunch						
2PM	Laundry	DRC	History	DRC	History	DRC	Study Group
3PM	Laundry	Chem.	History	Chem.	History	Chem.	Study Group
4PM	Study	Study			Study		Study Group
5PM	Study	Study	Study			Study	
6PM		Dinner	Dinner	Dinner	Dinner	Dinner	Shower
7PM	Dinner w/friends		Study		Study		Dinner
8PM		Read	Read	Read	Read	Read	
9PM		Read	Read	Read	Read	Read	Movies
10PM		Brush/ Bed	Brush/ Bed	Brush/ Bed	Brush/ Bed	Brush/ Bed	

⬇ WEEKLY PLANNER

Fill in the weekly planner for your week ahead.

	Sun	Mon	Tues	Wed	Thurs	Fri	Sat
7AM							
8AM							
9AM							
10AM							
11AM							
12PM							
1PM							
2PM							
3PM							
4PM							
5PM							
6PM							
7PM							
8PM							
9PM							
10PM							

DAILY

Once you have identified what needs to be accomplished each week, it is in your best interest to narrow the focus even more so you can see what needs to be in focus each day. This may be a time commitment every morning that could interfere with an additional 30 minutes of sleep, but beginning each day focusing on organization will make each day more manageable. The feeling of being overwhelmed happens when students get behind and feel that they can't catch up. The possibility of getting behind is lessened with the added focus on organization.

Students with ASD could need additional frequent reminders to complete hygiene tasks, eat healthily, take medications, stay on task, and to have a social outlet. By outlining the daily tasks each morning, students will be able to take more control of their executive functioning difficulties to have a more successful day.

Students with ASD should not only plan for academic requirements and study time, but should also plan social activities with peers. This is often an area that gets overlooked with students with ASD, but getting involved socially can help students develop a sense of belonging within their campus culture. Also, if you approach your planning system as a commitment, then once something is written down, it becomes a commitment that has to be completed. If something needs to be taken off the schedule, it should be rescheduled for another time instead of deleted from the plan.

Table 2.2 Daily Planner Example

Monday 4/29/2013	
7AM	Wake up, shower, brush teeth
8AM	Breakfast
9AM	English
10AM	Read History
11AM	History
12PM	Lunch
1PM	Free computer time
2PM	Chemistry Lab
3PM	Chemistry Lab
4PM	Chemistry Lab
5PM	Dinner with Roommate
6PM	Study Math
7PM	Study Math
8PM	Free computer time
9PM	CAB movie night in Student Park
10PM	CAB movie night in Student Park

DAILY PLANNER

Fill in the daily planner to plan your day tomorrow.

	Date:
7AM	
8AM	
9AM	
10AM	
11AM	
12PM	
1PM	
2PM	
3PM	
4PM	
5PM	
6PM	
7PM	
8PM	
9PM	
10PM	

USING TECHNOLOGY TO PLAN

Most college students have a strong grasp of how to use technology. The majority of college students come to campus with any combination of computer, laptop, tablet, MP3 player, and smart phone. Each of these devices has the capacity to serve as a planning system. While students may not be able to make use of these devices to set up the semester planning system, they most certainly can use them for weekly and daily planning. These pieces of technology can often be linked with each other so any updates on one will automatically be updated to the other. Many students are comfortable using these devices on a daily basis; this is a way to introduce a reliable way of organizing their lives using tools that appeal to them.

Students with ASD often need visual and auditory reminders to stay focused and work towards task completion. These pieces of technology can also serve as a reminder system. Auditory and visual reminders can be set to make sounds, vibrate, and give a textual reminder of upcoming commitments. These reminders can be set for as far out as 24 hours or as close to the time commitment as 15 minutes. Students who use planning systems that they are comfortable with will inevitably stay more committed to the system.

Review the technology you use and identify the steps to set reminders for yourself. Which device do you use regularly enough that can serve as a reminder tool?

_____

_____

_____

_____

_____

_____

_____

_____

_____

_____

LESSON 2: MANAGING TIME AND ASSIGNMENTS

Once you have recognized and mastered your preferred planning method, you can use your organization skills to manage your time and the academic demands of college. Setting reminders and creating "To Do" lists are two options to help guide your time. Learning to use these kinds of tools allows you to work and study efficiently.

"TO DO" LISTS

Some students with ASD can become hyper-focused on an area of interest or a subject they feel passionately about and their other coursework can be ignored. Creating a "To Do" list on paper or on a smart phone is an option that allows you to check off the finished items and still have a visual reminder of what you have to accomplish. As you use "To Do" lists, you can also monitor the tasks you complete by highlighting through all completed tasks. Highlighting allows you to check off items which have been completed, but still see what has been accomplished.

Many students with ASD have benefitted greatly from the use of either daily or weekly "To Do" lists. These lists are highly detailed and can help with setting the priorities of the week. By outlining the assignments, tests, and study hours needed, you can keep in control of all your requirements.

An additional piece of work that is vital is prioritizing these tasks. To help organize the tasks for completion you can prioritize by using the following numbering system: (1) High priority: must be done today; (2) Priority: should be done today; (3) Low priority: doesn't have to be done today, but it would be good to get this completed; (4) Move to the next day.

Using your preferred planning system and schedule, work to create daily, weekly, or semester "To Do" lists and make a habit of marking off your accomplishments. If you have a life coach, they can help you with this. Using a weekly study sheet to log your study hours is a great way to start working on assignment lists. Strategies like these provide invaluable support for busy students on the spectrum as they navigate college life.

Table 2.3 Detailed "To Do" List Example

Date	Classes	Assignments (with due dates)	Progress	Completed/Submitted
8/20 Friday	History (9–9:50) Math (11–11:50) Chemistry (1–1:50) DRC Check-In	Organize syllabus Organize syllabus Organize syllabus Pick up accommodation letters (these go to each professor)		Do you have a folder for each class? Yes/No Printed your letters? Yes/No Have you checked the online site? Yes/No
8/21– 8/22 Sat./Sun.				Do you have everything you need for your classes? Yes/ No
8/23 Monday	History (9–9:50) Math (11–11:50) Chemistry (1–1:50)	Read Ch. 1 Create Math lab account Organize folder & read Ch. 1		Turned in accommodation letter (after each class) History: Yes/ No Math: Yes/ No Chemistry: Yes/No Have you reviewed each of the syllabi? Yes/No
8/24 Tuesday	Music (10:50– 12:05) MoSAIC (3–3:50)	Sort out syllabus & turn in accommodation letter Introduction Week		Turned in accommodation letter (after each class) Music: Yes/ No
8/25 Wednesday	History (9–9:50) Math (11–11:50) Chemistry (1–1:50)	Print Ch. 1 PowerPoint (before class) Practice logging in to my Math lab Print Ch. 1 PowerPoint (before class)		Do you have Math lab and do you understand how to use it? Yes/ No
8/26 Thursday	Music (10:50– 12:05) Chem Lab (1:50– 3:05)	Read Ch. 1 (before class) Lab starts next week		
8/27 Friday	History (9–9:50) Math (11–11:50) Chemistry (1–1:50)	QUIZ proctor form due (Quiz 8/30) Section 1 (3 parts) (due 9/20 by midnight) Ch. 1 practice problems (#1–15)		Did you turn in your proctor form? Yes/ No
8/28- 8/29 Sat./Sun.	Study for History quiz (notes, book, handouts)			Have you studied for quiz? Yes/ No Are you prepared for the upcoming week? Yes/ No

DETAILED "TO DO" LIST

Use this "To Do" list to outline in detail what you need to accomplish this week.

Date	Classes	Assignments (with due dates)	Progress	Completed/Submitted

Table 2.4 Simple "To Do" List Example

Weekly "To Do" List	
Assignments:	**Priorities:**
Read Chapter 1 (Biology)	Due in class 8/23
Research Paper	

SIMPLE "TO DO" LIST

Use this blank Simple "To Do" List to outline what you need to accomplish this week.

Weekly "To-Do" List	
Assignments:	**Priorities:**

Table 2.5 The Myths and Truths About Organization Systems

Myth	Truth
I can already remember everything.	Your brain will only hold so much before you start to forget important things.
I have never needed a planner before.	College is very different from high school and you will need to remember more on your own.
I don't have the time to put information into a planner.	Taking some time in the beginning to organize everything will save time in the end.
I haven't forgotten assignments before.	Again, in college there are many more things to remember. It is better to plan first, rather than wait until you start to forget things.
I don't want to have to carry another thing.	You can do this on your phone or computer so you don't have to carry anything additional.
Planners have never worked for me before.	That doesn't mean it won't work this time.

LESSON 3: SETTING GOALS

Goals provide students with focused direction, help with prioritizing, and realistic steps toward a future accomplishment. Students typically come to college with the goal of graduating prepared to enter the workplace. Graduation is a long-term goal achieved by a series of short-term goal achievements. It is important to set realistic goals that are readily achievable. You should begin the goal-setting process by setting a timeline for completion. If the long-term goal is to make an "A" in a certain course, then understand that this goal can be reached by achieving a series of short-term goals like earning an "A" on each of your semester exams and papers.

When you set a goal, think about potential barriers to this goal and consider alternative paths to accomplishment. Barriers and roadblocks can happen, but the key is to be flexible and identify ways to adjust your efforts or deadline. Recognize that roadblocks do not reflect on your abilities as a student. They merely present situational barriers that you can get past with flexibility. Lastly, celebrate when you complete your goal. It is important to encourage yourself to continue the goal-setting process and looking forward to a celebration once the goal has been completed is an effective way to do so.

Students with ASD could benefit from setting short-term goals that help them work towards the long-term goals that they often lose sight of. Weekly short-term goals can serve as direction as well as points of celebration for accomplishments. Goals for students with ASD should include academic, personal, and social goals so they do not become stagnant in any one area of their lives. Finally, these weekly goals can be used as an honest self-evaluation system so you can monitor your progress. You should evaluate yourself frequently and honestly so suggestions and improvements can be made. Using weekly goals to evaluate progress is a way to stay focused on progress.

What is your long-term goal for each of the following areas? Why is this goal important?

Academic:

_____

_____

_____

_____

Personal:

_____

_____

_____

_____

Social:

_____

_____

_____

_____

What are some potential barriers to achieving your goals?

_____

_____

_____

_____

What can you do to overcome these barriers to success?

_____

_____

_____

_____

BACK TO BASICS

Consider these questions as you prepare to rate yourself on the BASICS of organization in academics.

B	**Behavior**	What are you doing to actively become organized? What planning systems are you committed to using? What myths about planning systems are you disproving? Are you consistently using your planning system? Have you set and re-visited your short-term goals?
A	**Academics**	Are you attending all your classes on time? Are you applying organizational strategies? Are you keeping up with everything?
S	**Self-care**	Are you getting enough sleep? Are you eating healthily? Are you planning for your self-care activities? Are you keeping your space clean? What are you doing to make sure you are managing your stress level?
I	**Interaction**	Are you checking in with your support team? Are you planning time for social activities? Are you actively engaged in classes? What are you doing to get to know your roommates? Are you checking your email/blackboard daily?
C	**Community**	Do you feel like you belong? Are you asking for help when needed? Have you met anyone new? Do you know the names of any classmates? Are you involved in anything socially?
S	**Self-monitoring**	Are you managing your time? Are you accepting critical feedback? Are you managing your frustration level? Are you willing to see the perspectives of others? Are you advocating for yourself?

BACK TO BASICS: RATE YOURSELF

Take some time to evaluate yourself honestly on the BASICS. Think about what you have learned previously as well as what you have learned about organization, planning, and goal setting.

		Comments
B	**Behavior** 1 2 3	Comments
A	**Academics** 1 2 3	Comments
S	**Self-care** 1 2 3	Comments
I	**Interaction** 1 2 3	Comments
C	**Community** 1 2 3	Comments
S	**Self-monitoring** 1 2 3	Comments

GOALS

Personal:

Academic:

Social:

Chapter 3

COMMUNICATION IN ACADEMICS

Being able to communicate with the professionals on a college campus may be the difference between getting the needed support and "riding solo."

TOOLS FOR SUCCESS

- Using a syllabus

- Monitoring your progress

- Academic communication

    - Communicating with professors

    - Body language

    - Communicating through email

INTRODUCTION

Using effective communication strategies is an important aspect of a student's goal of navigating the college campus. Whether it is speaking with professors about grades after class, sending an email to make a professor aware of an absence, asking for assistance at the Writing Center, meeting with a group of students from class to work on a project, or working with a tutor, students can make the most of their academic experience when they utilize effective communication strategies. For students with ASD, learning different ways to communicate with professors, university staff, and fellow classmates can help to ensure that academic expectations and needs are clear (Wolf *et al.* 2009).

The first step in becoming a responsible college student is learning how to use the syllabus and why it is important. The information in a course syllabus is a sort of roadmap for the class. The professor is giving you the directions to the finish line and will often outline any potential roadblocks. It is up to students to make sure they read and understand the syllabus. One concern that students with ASD have expressed is the lack of clarity throughout the semester. The syllabus is what gives students that clarity they need. The syllabus also provides answers to the questions students do not want to ask, and is where professors will explain their preferred method of communication. Professors review the syllabus for each class on the first meeting day of the semester. It is vital that students attend the first day of class to go through this important information.

LESSON 1: USING A SYLLABUS

During the first class meeting time of each semester, each student will receive a printed copy or be directed to an online version of the course syllabus. This is the most important document you will receive from your professors. Learning some ways to utilize a syllabus for organization and communication purposes can help you manage the course. Provided on the syllabus is your professor's contact information including his or her office location, office phone number, email address, and weekly office hours. In addition, you will note that a course description with learning objectives, assignment details, attendance policies, and grading scales will be provided. Instructors also provide a tentative schedule for the coursework typically including an outline of topics covered, reading assignments, paper due dates, exam dates, and other important dates throughout the semester.

It is important for students with ASD to recognize that this schedule is tentative and may change due to the pace of the class. A professor may expand on topics or overlook topics depending on the involvement of the class. It will be important for you to prepare yourself for frequent changes to the schedule.

Keeping your syllabus available for your reference allows you to be aware of all of these components of your course. Use a technique such as highlighting or underlining key parts of your syllabus when you receive it. Note your professor's office hours, the grading scale, and topics covered in class. Then, using the tentative schedule provided, add the due dates of assignments and papers and your exam dates into your planner. Do this for each of your classes and you will have made a semester schedule to use each day, week, and month of the semester.

Another helpful tool from your syllabus is the grading scale. Your professor will have provided the information you will need to be able to calculate your grade. For every assignment or exam, write your grade on your syllabus beside the appropriate element of the grading scale. You will be able to use this to keep track of your grades in the class. Likewise, if your professor provides details about his or her attendance policy for the class, try to keep a tally of your missed classes to offer a visual reminder of how many times you have missed each class. For example, if you are only allowed to miss three class days without penalty, but you have missed one class, put a tally mark on your paper syllabus next to these instructions to help remind yourself that you have only two more classes you can miss without penalty. Using techniques like these will help you to incorporate information from your syllabus into your daily academic process.

Many professors will also include a reading guide in the syllabus for their courses. This will allow you to keep track of the required reading prior to going to class. In college, students are expected to read the assigned reading prior to class so they can be actively engaged in class discussions. Noting the required reading on your syllabus and marking the completed reading will help you stay on track with all course reading requirements.

HIST1010.01 − World Civilizations I (3)
CRN22722 − Spring 2013 − Dr. Professor

Office:	Brown Hall − 302b	*Tel.*	(423) 555-1234
Office Hours:	W 11:30am − 1pm*	*E-mail:*	My-Professor@navigate.edu
	(or by appointment)		
	* *subject to change*		

Course Description:

This course will introduce students to human achievements of civilizations and cultures in Eurasia, Africa and the Americas from the origins of civilizations to about the year 1000. Rather than taking a strictly chronological approach, it will focus more on the emerging cultures or traditions as expressions of their time and place. The creation of myths, gods and goddesses, Hellenism, Confucianism, Hinduism, Buddhism, Judaism, Latin Christianity, and Islam will be examined as value systems that gave meaning and organization to human life, reflected in political, social, technological, and artistic achievements. It will also show that these traditions constrained human alternatives, providing a kind of cultural hegemony within cultures, and that these traditions remain important in our modern world.

General Education Requirement:

This course fulfills a general education requirement in Cultures and Civilizations (Option

Class Hour: Brown Hall 401 − W 5:30 − 8pm

It is my goal to be as helpful to my students as possible, so feel free to drop by during offi call or email me to discuss any aspect of the class or how I can help you better succeed. A the night class, I am keenly aware that dropping by might be an issue owing to work considerations − if you email me, we can arrange something that works for you.

Objectives:

At the successful completion of this course, you should have attained a good grasp of the and main themes of world history and developed a sensitivity to the problems of worki primary source evidence. Additionally, you ought to have started building a repertoire of a skills which are required of an historian. The course will have fostered skills of independent and thought, of self-expression, and of working rapidly through large amounts of often material.

Evaluation, Course Dates and Make-Ups:

Lecture Sheets (Pass/No Pass)	100	− One per lecture; 12 deployed, 10 score, 10pts each
Quizzes	100	− One per lecture; 11 deployed, top 8 averaged/score
Mid-Term Examination	200	− 20 February
Final Examination	200	− 24 April, 7:45−9:45pm (N.B. time shift)

Thus, the calculation of your "Base Mark" will be the total of all of the above divided by the number associated with the weighted value of the four classes of assessed work (i.e. 6). The "Base Mark" may be augmented via additional points for active and informed class participation (to a total of +3).
A = 100−90; B = 89−80; C = 79−70; D = 69−60; F = <60.

FIGURE 3.1 SAMPLE SYLLABUS

This is your reading for the class. Always take this to class and stay up to date on the reading.

All four (4) classes of assessed work must receive a passmark in order to achieve a passing grade overall; if there are deficiencies, a failing mark may be awarded for the class as a whole.

The mark of "I" (incomplete) will not be awarded for this class save for extremely special circumstances. Everyone on the official roster will receive the mark which he/she has earned as of the date of the final examination, subject to the proviso identified above. Your decision to enroll and remain in this course indicates that you accept same.

Make-up examinations will be administered only with acceptable documented proof of inability to attend; requests for a make-up must be submitted within 48 hours of the exam date and the documentation produced at the next available period of office hours.

It is always good to know about the make-up exams.

Texts and Reading:

- Bentley, J.H. & Ziegler, H.F., Traditions & Encounters: A Global Perspective on the Past, Volume A, 5th ed. (Contact me if you have purchased a previous edition of Vol. A. for assignments)

- Hunt, P., Ten Discoveries that Rewrote History.

Additional materials may be provided via BlackBoard vel sim.

This professor uses an online account to manage assignments and documents for the class. If this is outlined in the syllabus you should plan on checking it twice a week for any updated postings.

There are assignments listed below for reading on a class by class basis; the TE text will help you to both prepare for the material presented in the lectures as well as an aide-memoire for revision. Being prepared ahead of time will be to your advantage as it will simply not be possible to succeed in this class by playing catch-up – especially given the class quiz structure. Plus, it's simple mathematics – we have a scant few weeks to get from the prehistory to AD 1000. Such a mass of information cannot be crammed into the night before an examination. The best path to success is to take notes as you read, take notes in class, and then synthesize the readings notes with the class notes – space is provided on the side of the PowerPoint presentation print-outs for this purpose to get you in the habit for the lectures which precede the mid-term though after that you must fend for yourself.

Attendance:

The professor clearly outlines that if you want to pass you need to attend class.

There is a direct correlation between regular class attendance and success. I state quite bluntly that you will need to master both the content presented in the assigned reading materials to pass the quizzes as well as the readings coupled with the lectures in order to truly succeed in this class's examinations. Additionally, the Pass/No Pass lecture sheets which you will complete at the end of each lecture will track your attendance and form a component of your final grade. Ergo, while you might choose to skip, which you may elect to do on any day barring the mid-term and the final, be aware that there are direct consequences. I view all students enrolled in University-level endeavors as being adults capable of making their own decisions as to how to best achieve their goals. This includes giving you the opportunity to achieve "Deferred Success" which, as you may know, is the new euphemism for failure. It is your choice.

N.B. if you fail to attend class, you will be absenting yourself from the opportunity to gain extra points via class participation. You will want to trust me when I advise you that even the brightest student will be glad of the potential for a points boost come the end of the session.

Statement on Plagiarism and the Honor Code:

You may take it as read that I know what cheating and plagiarism are; you should too. If you are in any doubt, consult your handbook. In short, don't try to pull anything. I have no desire to ever visit the Honor Court; however, I will feel no compunction about bringing any and all violators before them in order to protect the integrity of the other members of the class valid work towards their degrees.

FIGURE 3.1 SAMPLE SYLLABUS *(CONT.)*

ADA Statement:

If you are a student with a disability (e.g. physical, learning, psychiatric, vision, hearing, etc.) and think that you might need special assistance or a special accommodation in this class or any other class, call the Disability Resources Center (DRC) at 555-1236 or come by the office, 102 Red Hall.

As this class is at night and, as such, has a very different type of quiz/exam structure, students requiring assessment-based accommodation are encouraged to discuss their specific needs with the instructor very early on in the term if they are having difficulties.

Nota Bene:

The timetable as well as the other information contained on this syllabus is subject to change. It is the responsibility of the student to keep informed of such changes which may be announced, *inter alia*, in class, on BlackBoard, via email, carrier pigeon…

Course Outline and Reading:

Key: TE= *Traditions & Encounters*; TD = *Ten Discoveries (# = Chapter)*

Week 1:	9 January	– Enrollment and the Paleolithic
Week 2:	16 January	– Agriculture and its Impact: The Neolithic and Mesopotamia
		– TE Chapters 1 and 2; TD Chapters 9 and 3
Week 3:	23 January	– Ancient Egypt, Land of Pyramids and Pharaohs
		– TE Chapter 3; TD Chapters 1 and 4
Week 4:	30 January	– The Proto-Indo-Europeans and their Legacy, particularly in India
		– TE Chapter 4
Week 5:	6 February	– The Earliest Chinese Dynasties: the Xia, Shang, and Zhou
		– TE Chapter 5
Week 6:	13 February	– Meso- and South American Civilizations plus Oceania
		– TE Chapter 6; (optional TD Chapter 5 "outside of class" chronology).
Week 7:	20 February	**– Mid-Term Examination**
Week 8:	27 February	– Introduction to Empire and Persian Case Study
		– TE Chapter 7
Week 9:	6 March	– Imperial China
		– TE Chapter 8; TD Chapter 10
Week 10:	13 March	– NO CLASS (Spring Break)
		– TE Chapter 9 (you need something to read; it'll come in handy later)
Week 11:	20 March	– Ancient Greece
		– TE Chapter 10; TD Chapters 8 and 2
Week 12:	27 March	– Ancient Rome
		– TE Chapter 11; TD Chapter 6
Week 13:	3 April	– Trade and Religion in the Classical and Post-Classical Age
		– TE Chapter 12
Week 14:	10 April	– Aftermath
		– TE Chapters 13–16
Week 15:	17 April	– NO CLASS (Professor away)
		– Begin revision for the final examination
Week 16:	24 April	**– FINAL EXAMINATION**
		– 7:45-9:45pm (N.B. time shift)

This is a rough draft of a schedule for this class. It tells you what you should be reading, assignments and due dates and when class is canceled. Although this is subject to change, it is a good idea to add this to your calendar the first week of school.

Labeled with N.B. is "time shift" which means the date of this final is subject to change. Although most professors don't state this, it holds true for most classes. You will need to pay close attention in class so you will know when your final is.

FIGURE 3.1 SAMPLE SYLLABUS *(CONT.)*

SYLLABUS REVIEW

This should be completed using a syllabus from one of your current courses.

What is your professor's name?

_____

What is the best way for you to contact your professor?

_____

What is the attendance policy?

_____

What textbook do you need?

_____

How many total course points are offered?

_____

How are the grades weighted?

_____

_____

_____

What are your due dates? (Exams, papers, projects, presentations, assignments, etc.)

_____

_____

_____

What does your syllabus say about work that is submitted late?

_____

_____

_____

LESSON 2: MONITORING YOUR PROGRESS

College students are responsible for managing an array of classes, meetings, appointments, and social activities. Students with ASD might also have the added stress of learning new skills and practices during their transition to college life and independent living. Using a set of techniques for monitoring your progress can help alleviate the anxiety of the new environment. You can monitor your grades, academic standing, study habits, communication, and use of campus resources. Use your syllabus for each class to identify your priorities and use the syllabus techniques like tracking grades and attendance on the document. In addition, be aware of deadlines to add or drop classes, submit scholarship applications, test and quiz dates, and long-term project deadlines. Using your preferred planning method, keep track of these important items.

Understand that you have a support system at your campus and you can use the resources available to you. If you are having difficulty, ask for help. College is an environment of learning, so, naturally there is an element of instruction that students can take advantage of while they are on campus. If you have difficulty in a class, communicate your concerns to your professor, ask for tutors or an academic coach to help with organization, or research the resources that your campus offers for assistance, such as a Writing Center or Math Lab. Also, if you have a life coach, they will be there to guide you to these resources and to provide support each week.

LESSON 3: ACADEMIC COMMUNICATION

The daunting task of meeting individually with a professor for the first time is easier when students are aware of different ways to approach the conversation. Similarly, working on techniques for communicating with professors using email allows students to confidently address any concerns or questions they may have. Group work on projects and presentations can be exhausting for students with ASD, but learning ways to communicate with peers in the academic setting can help make group work a more positive experience. With an emphasis on monitoring your progress and working with a support team including your life coach (if you have one), communicating well in the academic arena can lead to greater academic success.

Students with ASD have expressed an intense discomfort in going to a professor to talk about a misunderstanding or a difficulty. Often times, students would rather ignore the issue and forget about it. Unfortunately, this approach can cause more difficulties in the long run. It is best to have the conversations before the confusion interferes with your progress. Being prepared for and practicing these conversations with someone who can give you feedback is essential for building this skill set. Because you are an adult, your parents can no longer call your professor to help solve an issue for you. It is now up to you to communicate on your own behalf, and to work with your professors to create solutions.

COMMUNICATING WITH PROFESSORS

Working with your professor is an essential element of each class in college. You will want to understand how to communicate well with each of your professors in order to understand assignments, ask questions, voice concerns, and to disclose your need for accommodations. If you visit your professor and communicate your needs effectively, he or she will often give you the opportunities you may need throughout the semester. If you wait until the end of the semester to talk to your professor about a difficulty, you will probably not get additional assistance.

At some point, you may need to meet with your professor during his or her office hours. Office hours are times that your professor has set aside to meet with students, so there is no need to make an appointment to see your professor during these times. If the hours listed on the course syllabus for a particular professor conflict with another of your classes or appointments, you can contact your professor to make an appointment to meet at another time. Realize that professors, like you, are busy and sometimes may be unable to be there during the duration of their office hours. If this occurs, simply send your professor an email or speak with your professor after class to schedule a better time to meet.

Always be mindful of your professor's time. While he or she is there to guide you, there may be times when it is more prudent to discuss an issue with your professor using email. Office hours are set aside for all of the students your professor sees, so try to keep your meetings to a minimum length if you notice other students waiting to speak with your professor. You can always follow up with an email after the meeting.

Before meeting with a professor, one helpful technique for students on the spectrum might be developing a script or list of questions to ask. If you consider what issues you would like to discuss, preparing a script can help you make sure that you cover everything you need to discuss. This is also a way to avoid the anxiety students with ASD sometimes feel when communicating with a professor. If you have more than one question, write them down before going to meet with your instructor. You can refer to your questions during the meeting and take notes on the responses to ensure you understand. If you are confused, ask for clarification. Some tips for these meetings include always introducing yourself and telling your professor which of his or her classes you are taking, showing appreciation for your professor's time, arriving on time to scheduled meetings, listening to your professor, and using everyday manners like providing an introduction and saying thank you.

SCRIPTS

EXAMPLE

"Hi, Dr. Smith, my name is John. I am in your Tuesday/Thursday morning section of Biology 1110. I have a question about the topics that will be on the first test. Do you have time to help me identify what I should be studying?"

"Good morning, Ms. Peters. I am in your General Chemistry class and I am concerned about the lab portion for one of the sections. Because I have Asperger's I tend to have some problems with my fine motor skills and I am concerned about the safety when pouring chemicals in lab. Is it possible for me to partner up with someone and we can share the responsibility of the lab work?"

SCENARIO

You are in your fourth week of your math class and you still have not been able to access the lab component on your computer. You are beginning to feel very overwhelmed and are contemplating dropping the course. Develop a script for how you would talk about this with your professor.

_____

_____

_____

_____

_____

_____

Now that you have had some practice, develop your own scenario and present it to someone to develop a script together. This can be something that is a genuine concern or something made up.

_____

_____

_____

_____

_____

_____

_____

_____

_____

_____

_____

_____

_____

BODY LANGUAGE

Students communicate with professors in more ways than just words. Often, students non-verbal behaviors do not match their intentions, but the perception of their faculty member is what is important. What message about yourself as a college student could you inadvertently be sending to a professor through your non-verbal behavior in class? What is your body language saying?

Your Behavior	Your Intention	Your Professor's Interpretation
Sitting in the back of class with your laptop open	–Using a laptop to take notes. –Makes you more at ease to not look at people when they talk to you.	–Disengaged from the class. –Not interested in discussion. –Spending time on Facebook or something else.
Head on desk during lecture	–Easier to process information without visual distractions. –The flickering lights may give you a headache.	–Lazy. –Partied the night before. –Uninterested. –Disrespectful.
Repeating what professor says	–Seeking clarification. –Helps processing.	–Student is mocking. –Trying to prove professor wrong. –Wasn't listening.
Frequently challenging professor	–Want to display knowledge of the subject. –Want to learn everything possible about the subject.	–Trying to prove professor wrong. –Mocking the professionalism of professor. –Trying to be the professor.
Asking too many questions	–Seeking clarification.	–Trying to monopolize the class time. –Trying to make professor look bad.

COMMUNICATION THROUGH EMAIL

If you need to communicate with a professor using email, there are techniques that are useful to learn and remember when you are drafting your message. Some common situations that would be appropriate for sending an email might be informing your professor that you are sick and will not be attending class, asking for clarification on course assignments, or setting up an office appointment. First, provide a message subject that includes the title of your class (e.g. Hist1020-1). When addressing your professor, always use his or her last name and the title given on your syllabus. Many of your professors will have Ph.D. after their last name and should be addressed with "Dr. [Last Name]" when sending an email. If you are unsure which educational title to give in an email, "Professor [Last Name]" is your best option.

The body of your email should include the course to which you are referring, and a description of your concern or request. As you close the email message, show appreciation to your professor for his or her time as you would during an office meeting. Sign the email with your full name. If you have a life coach, you can practice drafting emails or going over your script with them before communicating with your professor.

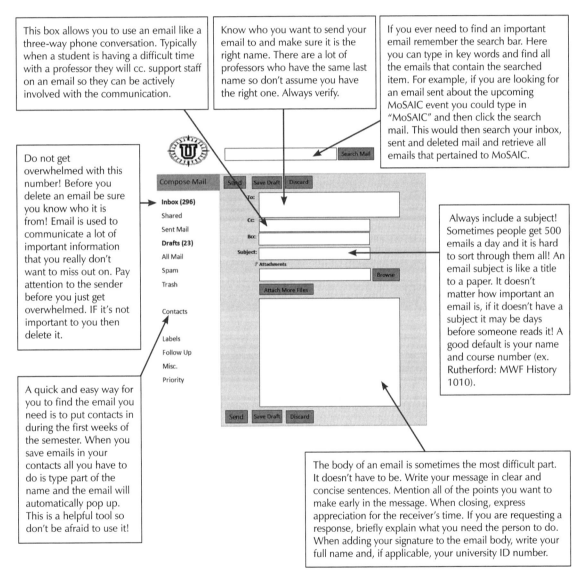

FIGURE 3.2 THE ART OF EMAIL COMMUNICATION

EMAILING YOUR PROFESSOR

Fill in the template below to practice asking your professor to set up an appointment.

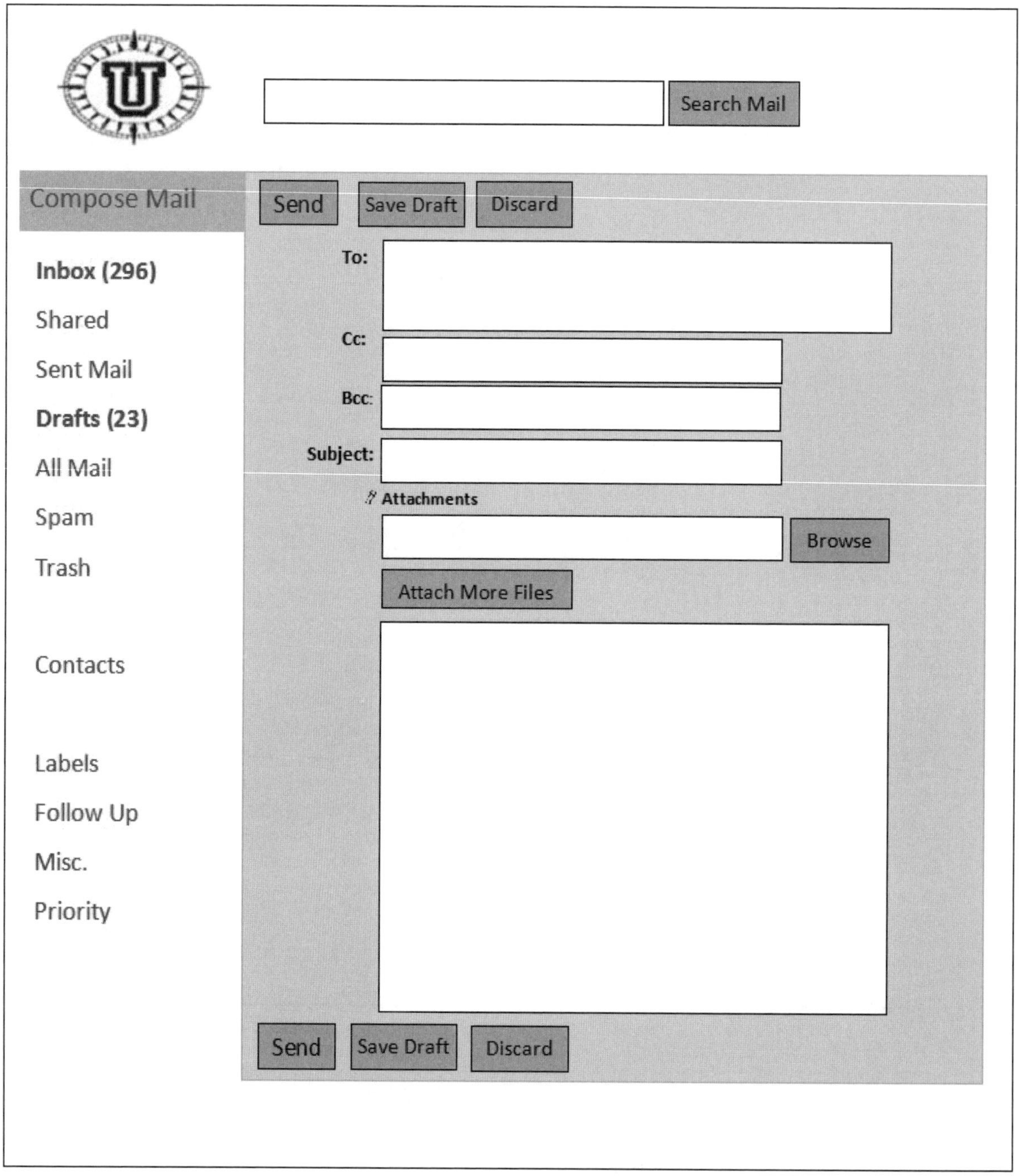

	Search Mail

Compose Mail   Send   Save Draft   Discard

Inbox (296)   To:
Shared
Sent Mail   Cc:
Drafts (23)
All Mail   Bcc:
Spam   Subject:
Trash
                     ⫴ **Attachments**
                                                Browse
                     Attach More Files
Contacts

Labels
Follow Up
Misc.
Priority

                     Send   Save Draft   Discard

FIGURE 3.3 TEMPLATE FOR AN EMAIL

BACK TO BASICS

Consider these questions as you prepare to rate yourself on the BASICS of communication in academics.

B	**Behavior**	Are you trying to effectively communicate with the people around you? Are you considering how they may interpret your message? Are you respectful in your communication with faculty and staff? Are you regularly checking your email? Have you set and re-visited your short-term goals?
A	**Academics**	Are you communicating with your professors if you will miss class? Are you monitoring how much you communicate with your professor? Do you understand all components of your syllabus? Do you know the best way to contact your professors? Are you keeping up with everything?
S	**Self-care**	Are you getting enough sleep? Are you eating healthily? Are you communicating your needs or points of confusion with your life coach, if you have one? What are you doing to make sure you are managing your stress level?
I	**Interaction**	Are you checking in with your support team? Are you planning time for social activities? Are you actively engaged in classes? What are you doing to get to know your roommates? Are you checking your email/blackboard daily?
C	**Community**	Do you feel like you belong? Are you asking for help when needed? Have you met anyone new? Do you know the names of any classmates? Are you involved in anything socially?
S	**Self-monitoring**	Are you checking and responding to your email twice daily? Are you accepting critical feedback? Are you managing your frustration level? Are you willing to see the perspectives of others? Are you advocating for yourself?

BACK TO BASICS: RATE YOURSELF

Take some time to evaluate yourself honestly on the BASICS. Think about what you have learned previously as well as what you have learned about communication strategies in academics.

B	**Behavior** 1 2 3	**Comments**
A	**Academics** 1 2 3	**Comments**
S	**Self-care** 1 2 3	**Comments**
I	**Interaction** 1 2 3	**Comments**
C	**Community** 1 2 3	**Comments**
S	**Self-monitoring** 1 2 3	**Comments**

GOALS

Personal:

Academic:

Social:

Chapter 4

ORGANIZATION IN LIFE

The state of our environment around us is often a reflection of the state of our mind.

TOOLS FOR SUCCESS

- Medical health

- Daily habits

- Self-care

  ○ Sleeping habits

  ○ Develop healthy eating habits

  ○ Eating well and excercise

  ○ Hygiene and cleanliness

  ○ Scheduling self-care

- Know your resources

INTRODUCTION

Independent living associated with college life requires students to manage their medical health, keep track of their everyday items, self-monitor their hygiene and personal well-being, and to establish a routine that works for them without daily help and reminders from home. Especially if students are taking medications prescribed by a doctor, taking care of one's health is very important to success in college. Also, students need to take their personal well-being seriously by practicing daily self-monitoring. Being familiar with resources on campus like the dining hall, student health services, and the Disability Resource Center for students is an essential part of students' goal of staying organized and prepared to take care of their overall well-being. Students with ASD can typically benefit from creating a structured routine set of habits that will help them manage the responsibilities of college.

LESSON 1: MEDICAL HEALTH

With all of the assignments and meetings to think about each day, it is possible that you could benefit from strategies for managing the additional concern of medication and appointments with doctors or other health professionals. When you are prescribed medication, recognize that you are independently responsible for not only taking it as prescribed, but also keeping it secure and safe. Use a weekly pill box to hold your medication for each day, and keep track of the times each day that you should be taking each medication. Use your planning system to remind yourself throughout the day. A helpful tool for remembering when to take your medicine is setting an alarm or reminder on your cell phone or wristwatch. When it is time to refill your prescription, a local pharmacy can help you get the medication you need.

Medication should be stored in a private place only you can access, like your bedroom, especially if you live in on-campus dorms. Medication is prescribed only when necessary for your health, so being responsible with it is being responsible for yourself. Many medications prescribed to people with ASD are similar to those prescribed to people with ADD. These tend to be the prescriptions that are often stolen and sold to people who take them recreationally and do not genuinely need them to focus. This is particularly difficult to manage on a college campus. If you take any stimulant or non-stimulant medication that is typically prescribed to help with the effects of ADD, please locate a private place in your room to store the prescription, and consider bringing a lock box to campus to secure your medication.

Often, people with ASD take many medications throughout their childhood. When they get to college and start living more independently, they occasionally decide that they want to stop taking their medication and start doing everything on their own. This may sound like a good idea, but any time you stop medication, you should do so under the supervision of a physician. Medications have many potential side effects, both when you start them, as well as when you stop. If you just stop taking medication on your own, you could experience a downward spiral that could lead to many negative side effects.

You can use Figure 4.1(a and b) to identify what you could experience as an upward spiral when you take your medications as prescribed. Conversely, you can also determine what the downward spiral may be like if you choose not to take your medication as prescribed. For each of the five identified descriptors in the loops of the spiral, identify what you feel, what others say about you, how you may react to what others say, and the potential outcome in Tables 4.1c and d. See Tables 4.1a and b for examples of what someone might write in this exercise.

Table 4.1a You Don't Take Medication as Prescribed Example

What do you feel?	What are others saying?	What is your reaction to what others say?	Possible outcomes?
Happy, free.	Did you take your medication? You're too loud. You've got a lot of energy.	This is just me, why do I need medication? I'm having fun. You don't know what it's like to take a pill every day.	Forgetful. Get in trouble. Unproductive.

Table 4.1b You Take Medication as Prescribed Example

What do you feel?	What are others saying?	What is your reaction to what others say?	Possible outcomes?
Focused, less anxious, directed.	Did you take your medication? You are getting a lot done today. Look at that focus.	Frustration (why is my success based on a pill?). I'm accomplishing a lot though.	Getting your work done. Able to have free time. People like to be around you. Good grades.

Table 4.1c You Don't Take Medication as Prescribed

What do you feel?	What are others saying?	What is your reaction to what others say?	Possible outcomes?

Table 4.1d You Take Medication as Prescribed

What do you feel?	What are others saying?	What is your reaction to what others say?	Possible outcomes?

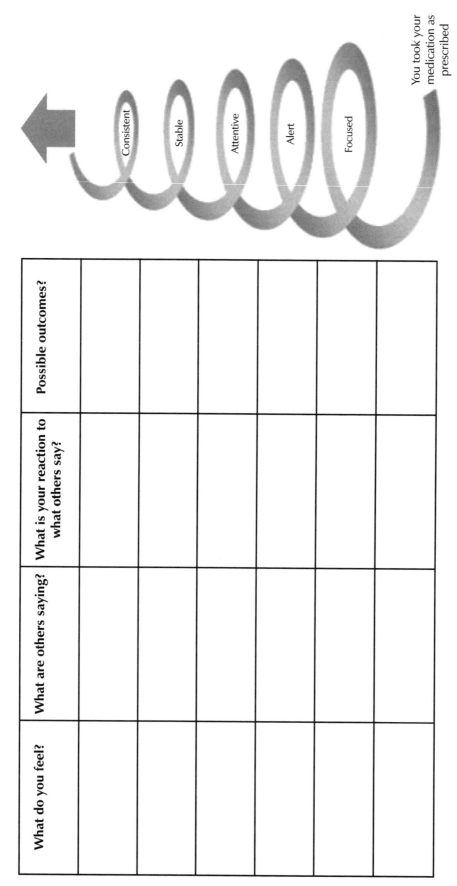

What do you feel?	What are others saying?	What is your reaction to what others say?	Possible outcomes?

Consistent

Stable

Attentive

Alert

Focused

You took your medication as prescribed

FIGURE 4.1A WHEN YOU TAKE YOUR MEDICATION AS PRESCRIBED

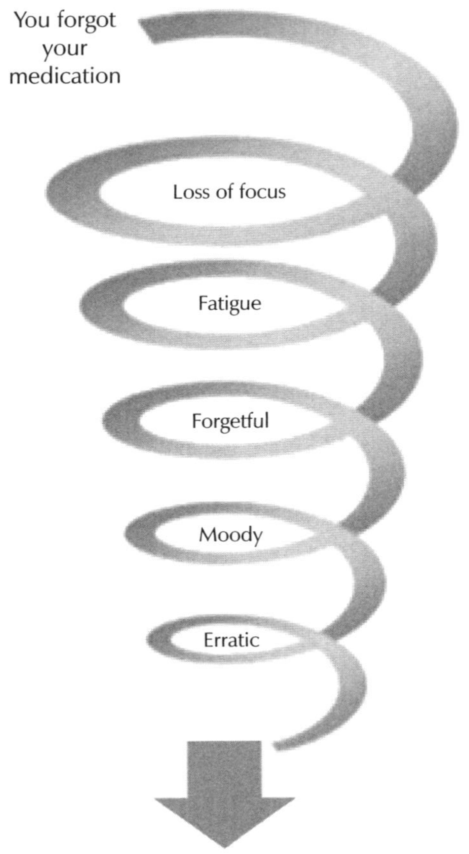

What do you feel?	What are others saying?	What is your reaction to what others say?	Possible outcomes?

You forgot your medication

Loss of focus

Fatigue

Forgetful

Moody

Erratic

FIGURE 4.1B WHEN YOU DON'T TAKE YOUR MEDICATION AS PRESCRIBED

LESSON 2: DAILY HABITS

Think about the items you use every day. Every time you leave your room, what are the things you must have with you at all times? Now, consider ways that you can be sure you have these things without someone at home reminding you to take them with you. Part of college life is being responsible for your everyday items—your keys, cell phone, school ID, cash or credit cards, and a backpack with your schoolwork. Find a place in your room for these things, and leave them there when you enter your room each time. A good idea is a table or basket beside your door. Then, when you leave your room, you will know where these items are and you will remember to take them with you and lock your door behind you. Making this a daily habit, along with your health and hygiene habits, will help you focus on other parts of college life such as academics and social activities.

People with ASD may struggle with remembering all they need when working through the transition to college. As this is your first venture into adulthood, it will be vital for you to prepare a system to help you remember what you need each day and where to keep these items so you don't forget them. Typically, your mom or dad have been able to help you if you lose your keys, your identification, or your credit card, but when you are at college, you will need to solve these issues either on your own, or with the help of your support system. To help you start thinking about what you need daily, develop a list to hang by your door. It may look like this:

DAILY NEEDS

- Keys

- Identification

- Wallet/purse

- Cell phone

- Medication

- Meal card

- Planner

CLASS NEEDS

- Backpack

- Textbooks

- Notebooks

- Pens and pencils

- Calculator
- Laptop/tablet

OTHER NEEDS

- Snacks
- Toothbrush
- Gym clothes
- Reminder cards

If you happen to lose something, it will be very important for you to know who to contact to solve the issue. Identify who to contact and the appropriate numbers to use to solve your problem. If you have a life coach, you could work on this with him or her. Consider the following important items you will use daily:

Room key

_____

_____

Meal card

_____

_____

Identification

_____

_____

Debit/credit card

_____

_____

Laptop/Tablet

_____

_____

Backpack with textbooks

_____

_____

LESSON 3: SELF-CARE

When you enter college there is no one who will be reminding you to take care of yourself, so this obligation is yours. Sleeping, eating, keeping your living space clean, and monitoring your personal health and hygiene are all factors of independent living in college. One of the easiest ways to hold yourself accountable for these parts of your daily life is to habitually schedule time for each. Daily self-care includes primary needs such as sleeping, eating, and managing hygiene.

SLEEPING HABITS

First, establish good sleeping habits. Assume that during the hours of between eight o'clock in the morning and six o'clock in the evening you are going to be busy with classes and studying every day of the week. In order to feel your best and perform your best academically, you need to create a pattern of sleeping that allows you to feel rested and ready for those hours. If you can schedule a short nap during the day, then you can do so as long as you can regulate your nightly sleeping habits as well. There will be times when assignment deadlines or social activities might keep you awake past your bedtime. Exercise a little flexibility when this happens as this can sometimes be a characteristic of typical college life.

Throughout our experiences with college students with ASD, we have seen students struggle with maintaining a good sleep schedule. This has been because students get caught up in their special interest areas or gaming and lose track of time. It is not unusual for college students to stay up late, but it becomes a problem when your sleep patterns become destructive and you start missing classes. If you are consistently staying up very late, and missing your requirements, you will not be successful in college.

EATING WELL AND EXERCISING

Similarly, be mindful of your eating and exercise habits. You can use your campus dining halls to find an abundance of options, and you may also be able to keep some food in your living space. The important thing is not only to keep in mind that you need to make sure you are eating regularly, but also that the food you consume has nutritional value. Consider making it a goal to eat fruit and vegetables each day, drink plenty of water, limit unhealthy snacks, and start each morning with breakfast. If you have dietary restrictions, then be aware of alternative food choices. Not only will you feel better with a healthy diet, but your academic performance can only benefit.

In addition to healthy eating habits, regular exercise is important during college. You can find simple ways to make exercise a habit. For example, take the stairs to your classroom instead of the elevator and ride your bike or walk instead of driving whenever possible. Most college campuses have some kind of recreational facility for students to use for exercise. Many times, college students with ASD do not enjoy going to the recreational center because it is crowded and noisy. The sensory difficulties with these types of environments tend to be too much to manage, but there are hours of operation that are not as busy. Try to find out the slow times and visit the recreation center to see if this is something you would enjoy.

HYGIENE AND CLEANLINESS

Taking care of yourself includes making sure that you are presentable and clean each day, so managing your hygiene is essential. To make sure that you are showering every day, schedule it into your daily plan. If you prefer to shower in the morning, then wake up a little earlier in order to do so. If you shower in the evening, make sure you leave time to do so and still be able to go to bed at a reasonable time that works best with your schedule.

Whatever your preference is, remember that your hygiene affects how you are perceived during college. Put simply, if you do not shower regularly, your body odor will make it difficult for people to be around you. The same point goes with making sure you use deodorant each morning and that you brush your teeth at least twice a day. Not only are these habits good for your health, but they will also help you be confident as you navigate the social environment of college. Keep in mind that while some students with ASD struggle with being mindful of their hygiene, others do not. All students in college need to find ways to monitor their hygiene, and building it into a daily schedule is the easiest way to make healthy hygiene a habit.

Along with keeping yourself clean, you must also keep your living environment clean. Keeping your living space clean, whether you live in on-campus dorms with a roommate, at home with your family, in an off-campus apartment with roommates, or in a single dorm room, is not only a matter of politeness, but will also keep you free from the implications of a cluttered living area. If you share a common area with anyone else, then you need to be especially considerate by cleaning up after yourself. No one else should ever have to do your dishes, pick up your trash, or wipe up your messes in college. You will not have a maid or family member to do these things for you. Learning how to independently keep your living space clean is a habit that will carry far into your future. If you share a bedroom with someone, then your part of the room should be kept clean and organized as a courtesy to your roommate. Try to schedule cleaning time in your weekly planning system. For example, you could plan to clean your bathroom area each Saturday morning and your bedroom on Sunday afternoons. The same principle is applied when you do your laundry. Just as you must keep your body and your living space clean, your clothes must be cleaned regularly. Learn where and how you will do your laundry and prepare some time each week to wash the clothes you have worn. If you need coins to operate a washing machine, be prepared before you take your clothes to be washed. Note these important kinds of regular cleaning habits in your planner and "To Do" lists and you will be able to manage your academic and social life as well as your daily personal needs.

SCHEDULING SELF-CARE

Lastly, part of self-care includes managing time for academic work. You are at college for an education, and despite all of the extra skills developed through the process of independent living, your academic work during college demands an appropriate amount of study time. You will earn the grades you deserve and the work you put in to each class will be reflected in your course grade at the end of the semester. So, just as you schedule time for sleep, cleaning, eating, taking medicine, and showering, plan on studying each day. Build it into your daily schedule—between classes, while eating breakfast, before dinner, or whenever works best for you. You can develop ways to make sure you give your academic curriculum the attention it requires. For example, if you like to watch TV before bed, then do so only after you have studied for a predetermined length of time. If you like to play video games on the weekends, then take frequent breaks to review and get ready for the week ahead. If you like to spend time outdoors, carry some note cards with you to study while you are outside. Your life at college does not have to be a constant study session, but you want to create a balance that represents your priorities. Since education is your primary goal during college, make sure your study schedule reflects that.

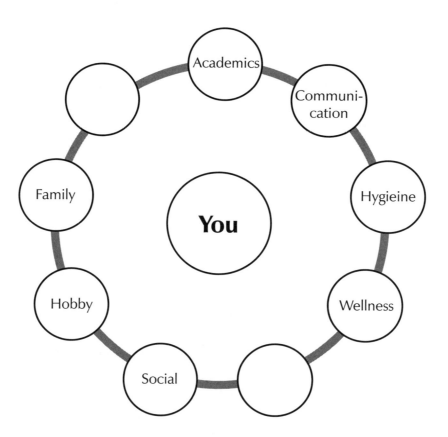

FIGURE 4.2 BALANCING IT ALL

"24-HOUR" PLAN

Every day you have 24 hours to plan for and use wisely. As a college student, many of those hours are taken up by requirements, leaving students very little free time to use as they choose. The following is as an example of how a typical college student might use their time in one 24-hour period.

Table 4.2 24-hour Plan Example

Personal		Total hours used	Remaining
Sleep	6		
Meals	3	**10**	**14**
Hygiene	1		

Academic			
Class	3		
Class reading	1	**5**	**9**
Homework	1		

Communication			
Check email	1		
Talk with profs	1	**3**	**6**
Discussion Boards	1		

Social			
Talk with friends	2		
Club meeting	1	**4**	**2**
Res Hall activity	1		

Free time			
Video games			
Fan fiction		**2**	**0**
Computer			
Comic books			

"24-HOUR" PLAN

As a college student, you will have many areas of your life you will need to balance. Consider the following activity as a way to establish balance. You are at the center of all the requirements in your life. At any time, you may be leaning towards one requirement more heavily, but that does not mean that you forget about the other areas that need attention. What requirements are in each? How would you fill in the open spaces?

Personal

Total hours used

Remaining

Academic

Communication

Social

Free time

LESSON 4: KNOW YOUR RESOURCES

Some of the common non-academic departments and programs on campus that provide resources to you as an independent college student include campus dining halls, a counseling center, campus recreation, student health services, a center for students with disabilities, an academic advising department, and a bookstore (Wolf *et al.* 2009). Knowing where these resources are located on your campus, hours of operation, and phone numbers will help you to take advantage of these kinds of support. Make a list of these resources and the information you will need for working with each. It might also be a good idea to introduce yourself to someone who works at each resource department in case you need to contact someone to ask questions or voice concerns.

Often times, students with ASD have not been highly challenged academically throughout high school. The level of academic rigor is likely to be very different in college. Although academic work may be manageable for students with ASD, the art of managing the level of academic expectations may be more difficult. It will be important for students to develop a system for managing their full-time job as college students.

A full-time job consists of at least 40 hours of work per week. If you are a full-time student, you should plan on spending no less than 40 hours each week on academic work. This time spent on academics combined with the new task of keeping life organized independently may become overwhelming. Knowing the support resources on a college campus will be vital to developing your system of support outside of your family. To help identify and locate these resources on campus, engage in this photo scavenger hunt.

 CAMPUS PHOTO SCAVENGER HUNT

To better understand the various support services on your campus, solve the clues, then locate the departments on your campus. Once you identify the office location, go to the department and take a picture of yourself or your group at the location.

1. You are running a fever and have a scratchy throat. Usually your mom takes care of you when you don't feel well, but you are on your own now. This place will test you for strep throat and give you the medicine to make you feel better.

   _____

2. You are feeling anxious about mid-terms and you are not quite sure why. Maybe you are letting your need for perfection get in the way of studying, or maybe you are worried about your final grade. Whatever the reason, the people in this department can help you manage your stress.

   _____

3. If you aren't sure about what class to take next in your sequence and you don't have an advisor for your major yet, where do you go to ask questions about your schedule?

   _____

4. You need to set up accommodations for your classes but you aren't sure what you qualify for. Visit this department to talk about the impact of your disability and request accommodations.

    _____

5. You are beginning your junior year in college and want to start building your resume. This department can help you build your resume, practice interviews, and locate potential employers while you are in college and right after you graduate.

    _____

6. You know that exercise helps you manage stress and helps you lead a healthy lifestyle. You also know that freshmen tend to gain weight their first year in college, so to avoid that, you can visit this place to work out.

    _____

7. Writing has always been a struggle for you, but now that you are in college, you have papers due for every class. Instead of getting overwhelmed, you can visit this department to get help on your writing process.

    _____

8. You brought your own laptop to campus but need to register it to be able to access the wireless network. This isn't something you can do on your own, so you take it to this department for assistance.

    _____

9. Your math class has caused you significant problems all semester and you are getting ready for your finals. If you don't do well on your finals, you may have to take the class again. This department can help you manage the difficult course content and locate tutors if you need them.

    _____

10. You are very interested in studying in another country when you become a junior or senior. You can visit this department to learn about the options you have for national exchange and study abroad opportunities.

    _____

11. You want to learn more about different cultures by participating in programs put on by different student organizations. This department thinks about multicultural issues and educates the campus about diversity and equality.

    _____

12. You want to learn more about feminist leadership and women's issues on your campus. This department educates about these issues and advocates for victims of domestic violence.

    _____

13. You lost your student ID and can't access your funds assigned to your account. This is where you go to replace your student ID.

    _____

BACK TO BASICS

Consider these questions as you prepare to rate yourself on the BASICS of organization in life.

B	**Behavior**	What are you doing to actively become organized? Are you managing your own needs daily? Are you following a good sleep schedule? Are you completing personal hygiene tasks daily? Do you have a reminder list of daily need items? Have you set and re-visited your short-term goals?
A	**Academics**	Are you going to class with all your materials daily? Do you have all your supplies for classes? Are you studying each day? Are you keeping up with everything?
S	**Self-care**	Are you getting enough sleep? Are you eating healthily? Are you planning for your self-care activities? Are you keeping your space clean? What are you doing to make sure you are managing your stress level?
I	**Interaction**	Are you checking in with your support team? Are you planning time for social activities? Are you actively engaged in classes? What are you doing to get to know your roommates? Are you checking your email/blackboard daily?
C	**Community**	Do you feel like you belong? Are you asking for help when needed? Have you met anyone new? Do you know the names of any classmates? Are you involved in anything socially?
S	**Self-monitoring**	Are you taking care of your own needs? Are you accepting critical feedback? Are you managing your frustration level? Are you willing to see the perspectives of others? Are you advocating for yourself?

BACK TO BASICS: RATE YOURSELF

Take some time to evaluate yourself honestly on the BASICS. Think about what you have learned previously as well as what you have learned about organization, planning, and goal setting.

B	**Behavior** 1 2 3	**Comments**
A	**Academics** 1 2 3	**Comments**
S	**Self-care** 1 2 3	**Comments**
I	**Interaction** 1 2 3	**Comments**
C	**Community** 1 2 3	**Comments**
S	**Self-monitoring** 1 2 3	**Comments**

GOALS

Personal:

Academic:

Social:

Chapter 5

COMMUNICATION IN PERSONAL LIFE

Knowing how to communicate effectively with your roommates and peers will help make your college experience less confusing and more meaningful.

TOOLS FOR SUCCESS

- Active communication
  - Body language versus verbal communication
  - Reactions
- Sharing the conversation
  - Small talk
  - Starting/ending conversations
  - Topics of conversation and no-go topics of conversation
- Personal space and tone of voice

INTRODUCTION

The differences between academic or professional communication and personal communication can be difficult to ascertain. Understanding the scenarios in which each type of communication is required and recognizing conventional communication guidelines will help. Students with ASD in particular can benefit from learning how to recognize differences and when personal communication is expected. What may be appropriate with a group of peers, for example, may be inappropriate in an academic context. Personal communication refers to that communication which occurs in a social setting outside of the academic and professional arena.

For students on the spectrum, social communication can be confusing and frustrating at times. Communication involves understanding another person's behavior and facial cues, positive and negative reactions, and tone of voice. These characteristics of communication are often those that drive the conversation for most neurotypical students. Students with ASD can learn to recognize these personal communication patterns that will help orient their own unique perspectives in accordance with those of the others during conversation. Understanding the purpose of and how to recognize social contact, body language, verbal conversation, personal space, "small talk," emotional non-verbal reactions, and the concept of shared conversation will be fundamental for college students.

LESSON 1: ACTIVE COMMUNICATION

As a college student, you will experience many kinds of social contact. A scenario as simple as passing another student on the sidewalk can be social contact. Working in groups for a class project, getting study tips from a tutor, having lunch in the college common area with a new friend, or waiting in line at the coffee shop are some other possible chances for social contact. Not all social contact can be planned for or expected, but that does not mean that it is something to dread or avoid. The potential of social contact is the possibility to forge new relationships, establish contacts, and enhance self-confidence. As a college student, there will be plenty of opportunities to practice skills that will help build your competency and confidence with social contact.

BODY LANGUAGE VERSUS VERBAL CONVERSATION

One of the most fundamental elements to any kind of communication, particularly one-on-one conversations, is reciprocal attention. This element ensures that the conversation progresses and is effective regardless of its intention. Even if a person is simply asking you to check your watch and tell her the time, showing her that she has your attention is the difference between seeming rude or seeming friendly. This small social contact does not demand a particularly large amount of interaction, but as a student you could reap benefits from practicing the social skills that are used during this kind of limited interaction.

When we are discussing communication, be aware that there is a difference between verbal conversation and body language. Verbal conversation is a spoken exchange with another person or group. But it is unlikely that an entire message is conveyed using words only during verbal conversation. Body language is often used in conjunction with verbal conversation to communicate. Since reciprocal attention is an important element of communication, interpreting both verbal conversation and body language is essential. Individuals on the spectrum can sometimes struggle with the concept of body language. Indeed, it is often difficult to interpret, but once this skill of interpretation has been developed, body language is less confusing and can even be useful in effective communication.

To examine this idea further, imagine a friend comes to you and shares the following statement: "I have some news to share with you." This statement alone can be interpreted in many ways. Her news might be something that makes her sad, excited, angry, happy, or scared. From the statement alone, the news she references is difficult to distinguish. If you consider her body language, however, you will often notice cues that can relay her emotional state to you without words.

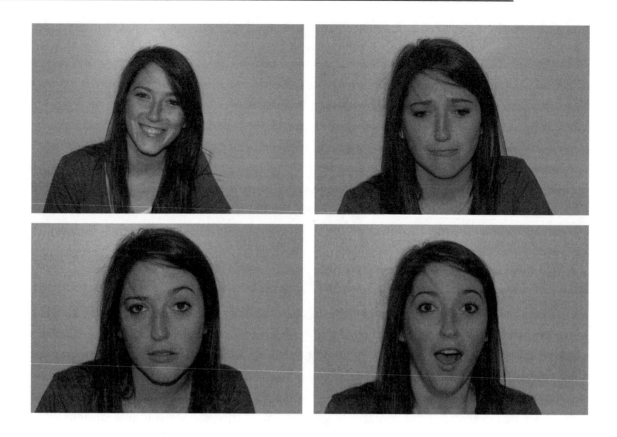

FIGURE 5.1 PHOTOS OF FOUR FACIAL EXPRESSIONS FOR "I HAVE SOME NEWS FOR YOU"

Can you think of similar statements that arc often paired with facial expressions?

_____

_____

_____

_____

_____

Other than facial expressions, can you think of other body language that could be a cue to an emotional message?

_____

_____

_____

_____

_____

Facial expressions are not the only way one uses body language to convey a message. Body posture, hand movement, direction of gaze, and even audible sighs are all incorporated in the term "body language." As a college student with ASD, it is important for you to value your social interactions and build a solid knowledge of how your own body language is perceived by others. It is difficult to have a conversation with someone who seems bored, inattentive, or closed off. Some common types of body language that give an impression of boredom, inattention, or lack of engagement include an indirect and wandering gaze, playing with one's cell phone, twirling around in a chair, turning one's body away from the speaker, slouching, or lying one's head down on a desk. While you may indeed be bored by a conversation, it is inappropriate to dismiss the person with whom you are speaking by engaging in one of these types of body language.

When someone is speaking, look at the person. You do not have to maintain direct eye contact for the length of the conversation, but look toward the person so he or she knows they have your attention. Turn your phone face down if you are distracted by incoming text messages or calls during a conversation. There is always time to check your phone or email or read once the conversation has finished. You could miss out on important messages when you disengage from conversations, and it is also likely to give others the impression that you do not care about what they have to say to you.

If you find that you are consistently bored by other people's interest in topics in which you have no interest, try to see communication as an opportunity to learn something new. You might find that you are interested once you are introduced to a topic someone else cares to share with you. A fascinating element of conversation is shared knowledge. As a student, knowledge is critical to your success, and any opportunity to learn during college has the potential to provide you with valuable knowledge growth. In addition, learning how to communicate well is essential to a college student's success, so every time you are able to practice communication, you are building that skill set that will provide guidance for you during college and beyond.

Recognize these same behaviors as they are presented from other individuals in personal communication scenarios, and use your knowledge of body language to notice when others are bored or disengaged. Students with ASD are not alone in displaying these common kinds of body language, but students on the spectrum typically struggle not only with being aware of their own body language and its implications, but also interpreting that of others. Learning how to notice the body language cues in others during conversation can help you recognize elements of communication that include when the other person desires to end the conversation, change the topic, or challenge a statement you have made. When we discuss the concept of shared conversation, this will be particularly useful.

Verbal conversation and body language help people communicate their thoughts, feelings, intentions, questions, and desires. The parallel messages from verbal and non-verbal communication can be complicated, but patterns do exist, and once you are able to recognize them, they can help you become a more skilled communicator during college and when you enter the professional field. As you recognize body language cues and verbal signifiers in conversation with others, you can begin to develop that sense of self-awareness that will make communication easier and more rewarding.

REACTIONS

Another component of interpersonal communication is the presence of reactions during conversations. As an extension of the discussion regarding body language, reactions are typical for almost any kind of communication. A reaction is often produced by the listener during a conversation when important statements are made. Imagine a roommate asks you for a reminder of the due date for an exam in a class you share with him. When you tell him that the exam is the next day, he stands up, shouts "WHAT?!" and starts flipping through his notebook frantically. This is his reaction to the information you have shared with him. By his reaction and body language, you can assume that he did not realize that the exam date is quickly approaching, and was not prepared to hear that the exam is so soon.

When discussing reactions, it is important to try to differentiate between a situation in which the information has caused a reaction, and another in which behavior has caused the reaction. Sometimes information is surprising, as in the case of the exam date, but it can also produce reactions like crying, jumping up and down, or shouting. It is even more complicated when you consider that sometimes people cry when overjoyed, shout when they are excited, or jump up and down when they are angry. Taken in the context of the conversation, someone might cry when they find out that they are going to be a new parent and they are overjoyed. At the same time, however, someone might cry when they hear that a family member is very sick. Reactions must be interpreted in the context of the information that is given in order to determine how best to respond to another person's reaction.

Occasionally, behaviors also produce reactions during conversations. For college students with ASD, it is important to remember that not everyone you are in social contact with will expect or understand some of the behaviors that you might exhibit during conversations. Consider a professor's reaction to a student who is disobeying a classroom rule by speaking over others without being called upon to do so. The information that the student is sharing is not the issue that creates a negative reaction; it is the disruptive behavior that has created a reaction. Be mindful of this as you interact with friends, family members, university staff members, and, of course, your professors. A reaction can occur because of information or behavior, so pause to recognize which can be causing it, and, if necessary, adjust your behavior to limit negative reactions.

LESSON 2: SHARING THE CONVERSATION

The dynamic of conversation is such that effective communication is often achieved through an exchange—sharing and receiving—of information. Monopolizing the conversation defeats this objective. While you may be very interested in the topic of a particular conversation, it is important that you maintain an awareness of others in the room, especially if you are speaking to only one person. You could be an expert on a subject, but the typical conversation does not require a lengthy and detailed explanation of a certain interest. This might be appropriate if you are asked for such information, but usually sharing general knowledge is more appropriate for casual conversation. Likewise, be aware of people's reactions to you during the conversation. If they display body language that suggests they are bored or disengaged, or if they stop looking at you, or start doing other things, then it might be a good idea to end the conversation or try engaging with them again at another time.

On the other hand, it is important that you reciprocate conversation. When someone looks at you, says your name, gestures in your direction, or walks toward you as they are speaking, it is likely they are speaking to you and expect some response. Since you will be in social settings during college, you could be occasionally overwhelmed and wish to avoid any social interaction, but engaging with someone who wishes to speak with you is a matter of developing essential communication skills. You will not always be excited to be speaking with someone who stops you on the street to ask for directions to his or her next class, but you will find that when you do stop and engage, you will be practicing skills that are beneficial in more serious and time-consuming conversations.

SMALL TALK

There are endless opportunities for "small talk" encounters—those often trivial conversations in passing—in a given college environment. If we consider how often students interact with other people on an average day, this is not surprising. Students pass each other on the sidewalk on the way to their next class. They stand in line with strangers waiting for their order of coffee to reach the counter. They sit next to new faces during class each semester, and they engage in what is commonly referred to as "small talk" about the weather, sports, homework, or any of an array of otherwise insignificant jargon to avoid silence and pass the time.

As a student with ASD, this might often be a point of frustration for you. It is difficult to establish communication strategies for planned conversation, and to be prepared to engage in unexpected "small talk" might not even seem worth the time. But, with a few tools to deal with these situations, you can navigate this social game. The first step is to be aware. Be aware of the people around you on the sidewalk, in class, in an elevator, or even in your dorm room. There is a chance that in any of these situations, someone might initiate a conversation with you about something that, in your opinion, is utterly pointless. Be assured that it is not an act of deception to engage in conversation about the weather if you do not care about the weather. You are not expected to be a meteorologist if someone asks you if you think it might rain. This person is just trying to be friendly. The conversation is not expected to develop into an hour of intellectual banter, but perhaps only about ten seconds of mere acknowledgment of the other person's existence in the same space as you. Smile, nod your head, say "yes" or "no," make eye contact, and you have done your part in this example of "small talk" social contact.

STARTING/ENDING CONVERSATIONS

The ability to start or end a conversation with someone is a task that everyone needs to work on consistently. This is not a struggle only for people with ASD. In fact, people refer to communication as the art of conversation. As with any other art form, being good at communication takes a lot of dedication and practice.

The first step in joining a conversation is to listen to what is already being discussed. How to listen to what is already being discussed can be a challenge because people do not like eavesdropping. Checking your phone, looking at your planner, or reading a book while standing in the vicinity of the conversation is a way to disguise that you are listening in an attempt to join the conversation.

The next step in joining a conversation is to pick information that you can share without going too far off topic. People often get annoyed if people take conversations off topic. If you listen briefly, then decide if you have any information to contribute to the topic, this would be a good time to join. If you don't have any information to contribute, this would be the time to walk away and try another conversation at a later time.

Once you have joined a conversation, the final step in the art of conversation is knowing when to end it. At times, people continue a conversation until it feels uncomfortable simply because they do not know how to exit. It is important to look for the established signs that the other person is ready for the conversation to end. As a reminder, those signs could include looking at their wrist-watch or phone, looking away from you, sighing, etc. If you are done with your part of the conversation, it is also important that you do not just cut the person off. Listening to the other person is also important in conversation, so allowing the other person to finish his or her point is vital.

This process is often difficult for people with ASD because they cannot read cues as easily as neurotypical people. People with ASD will want to finish their point of conversation and may carry the talk on far longer than the other person is interested. Conversely, a person with ASD may want to exit a conversation and may end it too abruptly, appearing to be rude. This is an art form that you will need to practice frequently with people around you who understand you and can give you feedback.

TOPICS AND NO-GO TOPICS OF CONVERSATION

One of the most interesting parts about interacting with people with ASD is the vast knowledge they may have about particular topics. This can lend itself well to the development of conversations if managed appropriately. For instance, if a group of people are talking about visiting a war memorial on vacation and a special interest area is the history of war, this knowledge can contribute greatly to the conversation as long as the person with ASD does not monopolize the conversation.

Alternatively, a person's special interest area may contribute negatively to conversations as well. If a person is very interested in something that is not age-appropriate, introducing information about that topic may negatively impact the person's social identity. For example, if a group of people are talking about going horseback riding at their family farm and a person with ASD joins the conversation talking about "My Little Pony" cartoons and toys, that person may be identified as having odd interests and may be seen as an outlier.

Finally, there are some topics of conversation that can be identified as "no-go" topics on a college campus. These topics of conversation may be directly related to a special interest, but can get you into trouble with campus police, Judicial Affairs, or worse. Although some people with ASD know a great deal about weaponry, killing, or bombs, these topics of conversations are "no-go" topics on a college campus. College officials do not take these topics lightly, so if a person talks about, writes about, or draws pictures of killing people, that person could be in serious trouble. Keep your special interest areas in mind when joining a conversation. If there is any possibility of someone interpreting these topics as threatening, keep them to yourself on campus.

Although you may not intend to offend someone in a conversation, another person's reaction to you is based on his or her perception of your statement.

INTENTION VERSUS PERCEPTION

Here are some examples of how an intention and perception by others do not match. Use the last two rows to write examples of when your intention in a conversation did not match the perception of the message.

Intention	Conversation	Perception
I want to share with the class my vast knowledge of weapons and weapon structure.	"Although people think you cannot kill a person with a small blade knife, that actually isn't true. If I wanted to kill you with my pocketknife, I would simply have to place it between your third and fourth ribs, push hard, then jab upward to pierce your heart."	This guy is really strange and I am afraid he is going to kill me.
I want to tell my classmate that I am interested in dating her.	"You are the most beautiful girl I have ever seen in my life and if you were my girlfriend, you would never be alone again."	This guy is obsessed with me and might harass me. He might follow me home and who knows what he will do.
My writing assignment for English is open to creatively write about anything, so I am going to write about bombs.	"…although the killer had the right idea, he would have been much more successful with his kill number if he had placed a bomb in the bathroom of the Engineering Building. He would have achieved mass casualties if he opted for a bomb instead of a gun."	This student is in distress and thinking about blowing up a college building. I had better refer him to Judicial Affairs so nobody gets hurt.

LESSON 3: PERSONAL SPACE AND TONE OF VOICE

If you stretch your arm out in front of you, the length from your fingertips to your shoulder is a typical amount of personal space that most people are comfortable with. This is often referred to as your "personal bubble." That doesn't mean you should stretch your arm out for every conversation; just use this idea to guide your distance from people. Of course, there are exceptions to this rule of personal space when you consider relationship status, personal affection, group gathering, physical space allotment, etc. For some people with ASD this can be difficult to remember, particularly when you are very interested in the topic of conversation.

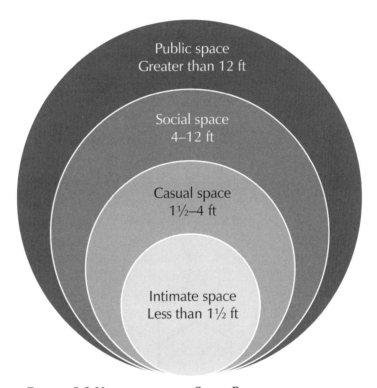

Figure 5.2 Understanding Space Requirements

Knowing the person with whom you are interacting is important in deciding how close to stand. Occasionally people with ASD get interested in the conversation and get very close to the other person. This could cause the other person to become uncomfortable in the situation. It is appropriate to ask the other person if you are standing too close if you are not sure if he or she is comfortable with your distance.

Similarly, it is important to keep your volume at a similar level as the person with whom you are speaking, and to recognize how patterns in tone can affect what is verbalized and attach it to some known or unintentional emotion. It is natural for people to get excited about the topic of conversation and raise their tone of voice, but if your conversation partner does not share the same level of excitement, your tone could seem threatening, rude, or overbearing.

Imagine being in a conversation with someone you have just met about a football game that was on last night. You don't watch football and don't even know the team the person is talking about. He gets very excited and stands very close to you, yelling loudly about the touchdown pass. In the end, he slaps your back to show his excitement. This could make you feel uncomfortable through the lack of personal space, raised tone of voice, or the slap on the back that could represent anger or excitement. All of this contributes to the confusion of social interpretation. People with ASD have a lot of great information to share, but it is so important to know the rules of social conversation. Look at the following figure and coordinating text boxes to help you practice these rules.

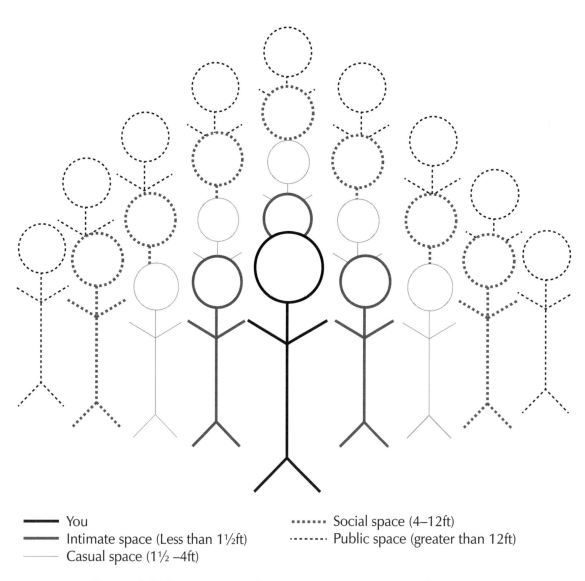

——— You   ······· Social space (4–12ft)
——— Intimate space (Less than 1½ft)   ······· Public space (greater than 12ft)
——— Casual space (1½ –4ft)

FIGURE 5.3 NAVIGATING THE SOCIAL WORLD OF PERSONAL SPACE

YOU

Space: You determine the size of your own personal bubble.

Who: You are responsible for how you feel in proximity of others. If you feel uncomfortable, examine why you feel that way and resolve the feelings.

Voice tone and volume: You determine what your personal level of comfort is in regard to voice tone and volume. What is your normal voice?

INTIMATE SPACE

Space: Intimate space is typically up to 1½ feet away from you in all directions.

Who: People in your intimate space could include your parents, other family members, best friends, boyfriend/girlfriends.

Voice tone and volume: In this range, the voice tone and volume should be regulated by how loud you need to be for someone in close proximity to hear, but not other people. You can usually use your normal voice tone with this group of people because they typically will understand your message regardless of the tone.

CASUAL SPACE

Space: Casual space is typically between 1½ and 4 feet away from you in all directions.

Who: People in your casual space could include casual friends, acquaintances, professors, staff of the university, roommates, and people at your table in the dining hall.

Voice tone and volume: In this range, you should be more mindful of the range and tone of your voice. People do not know you as well, so they can interpret your tone and volume to mean other things. You may need to raise your tone so others can hear you, but do not get too loud. With this group of people, you should focus on modulating your voice appropriately so they understand your message and don't misinterpret your meaning.

SOCIAL SPACE

Space: Social space is typically between 4 and 12 feet away from you in all directions.

Who: People in your social space could include peers in your classes, people at a performance, people at a party, or participants in a presentation.

Voice tone and volume: People in your social space will be having their own conversations, so your voice tone and volume should be highly monitored so your conversation does not interrupt the conversations of others.

PUBLIC SPACE

Space: Public space is any space over 12 feet away from you in any direction. In public spaces there are active crowds and the distance between people may be reduced.

Who: People in your public space may be people at an airport, at a concert, at a festival, or at a conference.

Voice tone and volume: You will typically be only conversing with people close to you in these situations, so monitor your volume so you do not interrupt others in this space and so others cannot hear your conversations if you do not want them to. Monitor your voice tone closely, because if your tone is misinterpreted in this space, you could get into trouble for being threatening.

Practice these personal communication skills and be considerate of how your behavior and attitude can affect others and influence their perception of you. With that said, however, understand that you do not have to sacrifice the idiosyncrasies that are attached to your diagnosis in order to be an effective communicator. Learn to recognize and model the difference between social conformity and your goal of social adaptation. It is not a matter of strictly adhering to the exact socially constructed behavior and communication rules that your culture has manifested. Instead, you are charged with finding ways to adapt to the social environment. Being self-aware and mindful of these guidelines as you independently navigate the social world of college will help direct you through an incredibly social period of your life.

BACK TO BASICS

Consider these questions as you prepare to rate yourself on the BASICS of communication in your personal life.

B	**Behavior**	Do you understand the personal space guidelines? Are you monitoring your tone of voice in conversations? Are you taking part in small talk with peers? Have you practiced starting/ending conversations? Have you set and re-visited your short-term goals?
A	**Academics**	Are you communicating with professors differently than with peers? Are you monitoring your conversations in class? Are you aware of the "no-go" topics of conversation? Have you offended anyone in your class with your topic or tone of voice?
S	**Self-care**	Are you getting enough sleep? Are you eating healthily? Are you planning for your self-care activities? Are you keeping your space clean? Are you keeping your own space requirements in mind?
I	**Interaction**	Are you checking in with your support team? Are you planning time for social activities? Are you actively engaged in classes? What are the personal space requirements of a peer? Are you checking your email/blackboard daily?
C	**Community**	Are you taking care of your own needs? Are you accepting critical feedback? Are you managing your frustration level? Are you willing to see the perspectives of others? Are you advocating for yourself?
S	**Self-monitoring**	Are you taking care of your own needs? Are you accepting critical feedback? Are you managing your frustration level? Are you willing to see the perspectives of others? Are you advocating for yourself?

BACK TO BASICS: RATE YOURSELF

Take some time to evaluate yourself honestly on the BASICS. Think about what you have learned previously as well as what you have learned about communication strategies for personal life.

B	**Behavior** 1 2 3	**Comments**
A	**Academics** 1 2 3	**Comments**
S	**Self-care** 1 2 3	**Comments**
I	**Interaction** 1 2 3	**Comments**
C	**Community** 1 2 3	**Comments**
S	**Self- monitoring** 1 2 3	**Comments**

GOALS

Personal:

Academic:

Social:

Chapter 6

STRESS MANAGEMENT

Everyone experiences stress and anxiety, but recognizing what it feels like and developing strategies to deal with it is what makes you a successful manager of stress.

TOOLS FOR SUCCESS

- Symptoms and triggers of stress
  - Identifying triggers (hot spots)
  - Low stress tolerance
- Stress can lead to anger: controlling your emotional response
  - Meltdowns
- Coping strategies to reduce stress
  - Reducing stress
  - Focused coping strategies
- Know your resources

INTRODUCTION

The transition to college life can be a stressful time for every student. Students are independently in a new place, with a different social environment, and they must be prepared for the academic challenges of college-level work. The unfamiliar aspect of college can be a trigger for stress in students with ASD. Students on the spectrum will find that being able to identify stress is essential. Once stress has been identified, the impact of its severity can be lessened by learning how to reduce stress and by taking advantage of the many resources available on a college campus.

Managing stress for a person with ASD may be particularly difficult. There are many cognitive processes that take place in the management of stress. These include recognizing symptoms of stress, identifying the stressful trigger, developing a coping strategy, and controlling the emotional response. Each of these steps is vital in managing a stressful situation independently, but it is more important that they all work together in concert. During a time of high stress, trying to manage all of these processes can be like playing a game of dodge ball. A person with ASD can usually catch or dodge a single ball coming at them, but as soon as someone throws more than one ball at a time, it becomes stressful. When several balls are being thrown from different directions, it is often unmanageable and chaotic. This time of uncontrollable chaos is what causes the stress and anxiety. Knowing how to create a sense of control can be the key to managing your level of stress.

LESSON 1: SYMPTOMS OF STRESS

Identify how stress feels in the various parts of your own body.

Cognition
*Lack of concentration
*Insomnia
*Wandering thoughts
*Fatigue
*Self-doubt
*Loss of memory
*Negative thinking

Behavior
*Shaking hands
*Fidgety
*Nail biting

Emotion
*Moodiness
*Racing heartbeat
*Depression
*Isolation
*Irritability
*Loneliness
*Short Temper
*Low self esteem
*Frustrated easily

Behavior
*Smoking
*Alcohol usage increase
*Avoiding responsibilities

Physical
*Headaches
*Muscle tension
*Chest pains
*Digestive problems
*Exhaustion
*Shaking
*Dry mouth
*Aches and pains

Behavior

*Pacing
*Fight or Flight
*Procrastinating
*Sleeping too much
*Sleeping too little
*Eating too much
*Eating too little

Behavior

*Hyper-focus on special interests
*Self-Stim behaviors
*Repetitive behaviors
*Hypersensitive to sensory stimuli
*Aggression

How does stress impact how you think?

_____

_____

_____

_____

How does stress impact how you feel emotionally?

_____

_____

_____

_____

How does stress impact how you feel physically?

_____

_____

_____

_____

How does stress impact your behaviors?

_____

_____

_____

_____

How does stress impact your behaviors or feelings associated with ASD?

_____

_____

_____

_____

IDENTIFYING TRIGGERS (HOT SPOTS)

The first part of the process of stress management is identifying the things that make you anxious, which are often referred to as triggers, and learning how your body and mind react. Stress may be difficult for a person with ASD to recognize because it is very different for each person. This makes it even more difficult to identify what is causing the stress. When we are unable to identify what is causing stress and what stress feels like, it can be far too easy for that stress to quickly escalate to anger. When stress escalates to anger, many more potential difficulties arise.

Everybody has triggers that produce stress and anxiety in their lives. For many college students, these triggers will be similar. A surprise test, a roommate who doesn't take care of the shared living space, the transition to a new environment, or a professor who is not helpful are some examples. College students with ASD often share these same triggers, but have others that neurotypical college students do not find stressful. These additional hot spots may have to do with sensory issues, feelings of failure, social rule confusion, feeling overwhelmed, or unpredictability in schedules. The ability to manage all of these things while managing your workload as a college student contributes to what we like to refer to as "social stamina." When your social stamina is running low, it becomes easier to get stressed out and angry.

Because college is such a social environment, college students with ASD may experience higher levels of stress and anxiety than other students or than they have typically experienced themselves. This difference in stress experiences could be attributed to a few factors. These factors are an introduction to understanding why you may be experiencing a different level of stress but, as always, the impact is very individualized.

LOW STRESS TOLERANCE

A college environment is a full-time sensory overload for the typical college student. Thousands of young people talking loudly, listening to music, crowded spaces, flickering fluorescent lights, and perfume everywhere. This environment can occasionally be difficult for a neurotypical college student to manage, but the hyper-sensitivities that often correlate with ASD make this environment incredibly stressful. Hyper-sensitivities occur when one of your five senses overloads with too much sensory input and creates a high level of stress. People with ASD often have hyper-sensitivity in one or more of their senses (Attwood 2006). If the flickers of fluorescent lights bother you, a typical classroom may make it difficult for you to focus; if smells bother you, you may need to eat your lunch outside instead of in the dining hall; if noises bother you, you may need to arrange to take your exams in an environment that is more controlled. Recognizing these hyper-sensitivities and setting up your environment ahead of time can help alleviate undue stress.

College students compete with others and with themselves every day. Students study more, write better, make flashcards, or meet with professors all to get a higher grade on the next test or project. This can be very difficult for college students with ASD. People with ASD tend to be somewhat rigid in their view of success; this is often referred to as their perfectionism. This narrow view of success can be the difference between a neurotypical college student celebrating a "B" on a test and a college student with ASD viewing the same grade as a failure. This view of success may contribute to the fear of failure often experienced by people with ASD (Dubin 2009).

Another aspect of college life that can contribute to the low stress tolerance experienced by people with ASD is the unpredictability of the college environment. At any time, a class can be canceled, a test can be changed, a threat can cause the evacuation of a building, or the menu at the dining hall can change. Whether these things are perceived as minor or major by your neurotypical peers has little to do with how you experience these events. Students with ASD often feel on guard in their environment with a need to control situations so there are no bumps in the schedule. They often experience great amounts of stress just planning for what could happen. This level of energy expelled by your sympathetic nervous system could deplete your mental and physical energy, making it very difficult to focus on the task at hand. Living in this constant state of stress makes it difficult to find the tranquil times and places to calm your senses and regain control of your thoughts.

Finally, one of the primary indicators of a person with ASD is monotropism. This is the idea that people with ASD process information in bits and pieces instead of seeing the big picture (Lawson 2003). Seeing the big picture and being part of the big picture is the primary way of life on a college campus. In a college course, the professor has a goal of teaching you information that you can then think critically about and generalize into other situations. In a social situation, recognizing the whole scene globally is necessary to be a successful social participant. Often, students with ASD get hyper-focused on the small details and miss the overall message which leads to confusion and frustration.

Although college is a highly stressful environment for a person with ASD, it is an environment that you can successfully navigate with practice. You can be a responsible manager of your stress by being very honest with yourself and others about what pushes you over the edge, recognizing when and where the triggers occur, identifying what stress feels like to you, recognizing when your stress level is approaching anger, and most importantly, developing a plan for how to manage the stress before it occurs.

As a college student, you are now an adult and it is your responsibility to manage your own reactions. It is the expectation that all students monitor their own behavior and adhere to the student code of conduct. Knowing what makes you feel stress and what can lead to anger issues will help you control your own behavior and keep you out of trouble.

SITUATIONAL STRESS TEST

Rate each of these situations according to how stressful they would be for you personally. Rate each with either 1 for very little stress, 2 for moderate stress, or 3 for very stressful. The items rated as 3 can be seen as your potential stressful triggers.

Situation	Rating	What about this makes it a trigger?
Your alarm didn't go off and you are running late for class.		
Your professor announces a pop quiz when you enter class.		
Your roommate ate all of your favorite cereal.		
The bookstore doesn't have the book you need for class.		
You have to walk through a crowd of people to get to the door of your class.		
The pen you are using to take notes has run out of ink in the middle of class.		
You lost your USB with all your homework and notes on it.		
Your roommate left dirty dishes in the sink.		
A professor just announced an in-class project that requires group work.		
A staff member at the university tells you that someone has complained about you.		
Your class runs late so you are late getting to lunch and the dining hall is out of what you usually eat for lunch.		

Your professor has asked you to stay after class to discuss something.		
Your friend has canceled your plans to go to the movie.		
Your professor left a note on the door that your class has moved to another location.		
Your in-class final has just been changed to a take-home final exam.		
Your neighbor is having a party and is playing music very loud late into the night.		
A person in your class is whispering and laughing.		
The fire alarm goes off in the middle of the night.		
Some people get into an argument outside the library doors.		
The seat you usually sit in is taken by someone else.		

LESSON 2: STRESS CAN LEAD TO ANGER: CONTROLLING YOUR EMOTIONAL RESPONSE

The stress of everyday life on a college campus could easily lead to anger if not addressed appropriately and in a timely manner. On a college campus, this behavior can conflict with the student code of conduct and can result in a student being asked to leave the school. It is vital as a college student with ASD that you develop a plan to manage your stress level before it leads to anger. As you become more stressed, you may speak to people harshly, increase your voice tone, or throw something or physically strike out at someone. Regardless of how you are feeling at the time of the outburst, or your intention regarding your behavior, when someone else is involved, the importance lies in how he or she perceives your behavior. If someone perceives you to be angry and threatening, your intention in displaying this behavior does not matter.

For example, if you are worried about whether a professor has received a paper you turned in to the departmental office and the secretary is not checking the mailbox as you ask, you may start to feel stressed and anxious about her lack of response. At this time, it would be good to rely on your stress management plan before your behavior turns threatening. If you raise your voice, enter the office uninvited, slam your fist on the desk, or approach the staff member in a threatening way, you could be referred to a Behavior Intervention Team and may be asked to leave campus. Even if you are not referred to this team for discussion, your reputation in the department will be tarnished and professors will always be on the lookout for your inappropriate behavior. This will overshadow your academic accomplishments in the long run.

MELTDOWNS

People with ASD have often experienced what we refer to as meltdowns throughout their lives. To others, meltdowns may appear to be simply childlike temper tantrums, but they are much more than that. Meltdowns occur when a person with ASD has experienced sensory overload or feel that their environment has become chaotic. After attempts to control the environment in many different ways, a person with ASD may react to the overwhelming amount of stress by losing control over emotions. These meltdowns are often frightening to others because they do not understand what is happening. They can often be loud, risky, or threatening, but are always difficult to manage unless you are prepared.

Meltdowns may serve a purpose for a person with ASD (Grandin 2011) and are often referred to as being cathartic. When a person become overloaded and overwhelmed, their brains trigger a need to purge information. As a child this may have resulted in full-blown meltdowns for some, or withdrawal and isolation for others. Knowing that there is a purpose for these meltdowns may make them less stigmatic for a person with ASD. Although there is a purpose for these meltdowns and there may be a need to allow this purge at times, it is your responsibility as an adult to manage where and when this happens. You are your own expert, so identifying how you feel prior to the meltdown occurring, identifying a safe place to go, and safe people to be around will allow this purge to occur without creating more chaos around you. This meltdown may serve a purpose for you, but should not impact others around you.

What are some of your identified hot spots? What are some cooling methods?

_____

_____

_____

_____

_____

_____

_____

_____

KNOW YOUR BOILING POINT: A SCALE TO KEEP YOUR COOL

Use the following exercise to determine some appropriate strategies for maintaining your composure in times of stress. Notice that different levels of stress will have various impacts on those around you, and you will need to figure out ways to assess your behavior. Reflecting on your levels of stress in a numeric way can help you identify where you are emotionally before you get into a troubling situation (Buron, 2007). This volcano image can help you understand where your stress or anger level is situated and how to manage stress at that level. List some possible strategies to cope with each level in the space provided in the boxes on the right-hand side of the image.

Extreme anger and potential for a meltdown. It is nearly impossible to think clearly at this level. Find someone you trust to help you calm down.

Expressing anger at this level makes others feel uneasy and afraid and may lead to you breaking the law.
Possible strategy:

Anger and extreme tension. It is difficult to think clearly here. Be very cautious with your anger and do not react with emotion.

You are still angry and discussing the matter now is not a good idea. Doing something physical can help.
Possible strategy:

Nervous and agitated. You could say something that would hurt another person's feelings. Consider leaving the situation to calm down.

After walking away, your mind and body have had time to relax a little. Talking to someone could help.
Possible strategy:

Uncomfortable and anxious. Moderate amount of tension.

This is a good time to think about and reflect on the situation calmly. Do not place blame on others.
Possible strategy:

Slightly uncomfortable and there is a potential for stress. Things are manageable, but keep your stress level in focus.

Everyday stressors impact everyone, but they are typically manageable.
Possible strategy:

5

4

3

2

1

SCALE FOR MANAGING STRESS AND ANGER

During a time of relaxation, reflect on how stress and anxiety affect you. Stressors rated 1 would be considered everyday stressors while a stressor rated 5 would be a situation where you may need assistance. Fill out the table below, identifying what your stress level may look like to others and how it feels to you. Finally, describe some techniques that could help you cool off during a time of stress or anxiety.

Rating	What does it look like to others?	What does it feel like to me?	What can I do to cool myself down?
5			
4			
3			
2			
1			

LESSON 3: COPING STRATEGIES TO REDUCE STRESS

During a time of relative calm, develop your stress management plan that you can rely on to help yourself out of stressful situations before you become angry and it becomes a behavior problem. Your plan should include identifying your triggers (hot spots), recognizing what your high level of stress feels like, recognizing how other people may see your behavior, and outlining stress-reducing choices (cooling methods).

STRESS MANAGEMENT PLAN

Use the table below to develop your plan. The first row gives you an example.

Hot spot	How it feels	How others see it	Cooling method
You get a bad grade on a test and your professor won't change the grade even though you think your answer was right.	Your chest feels tight and you are breathing heavily. You feel like you want to yell at the professor and tell him it is his fault you didn't understand.	If you yell and blame the professor, he may see you as disrespectful and threatening. He may ask you to leave his class.	Leave the classroom and go for a walk. When you have had time to think, write an email to the prof. with your questions and have someone review the email before you send it.

Developing this plan should be individualized and personal. This will be something you are responsible for controlling, but you can discuss it with your life coach if you have one (or with someone else you trust) to get feedback. As with any plan, if you do not see the value behind it, or commit to following it, it will not be useful. If you see no other value than to keep you out of trouble with professors and peers, then that is important enough.

REDUCING STRESS

As you learn to recognize patterns in the elements of college life that create stress for you, you will be able to more effectively reduce the impact of this stress. Reducing stress is often a matter of preparing yourself for those instances that you have identified as stressful situations. There are several methods for reducing stress. On a college campus, resources to help are around almost every corner. Be aware of the student service offices and departments on your campus like the Counseling Center, Women's Center, Disability Resource Center, and Academic Advising. These campus departments are staffed by professionals who are there to help you navigate the stressful college environment.

In addition to these departments, if you have a life coach, consult with them each week to discuss any stressful situations that you might have dealt with during the week. Your life coach is there to help you develop strategies for managing stress and he or she will also be able to guide you to communicate with other departments should issues arise that would be best discussed with more specificity by subject. For example, your life coach is not an academic advisor. While he or she can offer suggestions for classes, trained professional advisors are available to you to help reduce the stress related to academic planning. With that said, a life coach is a great place to start when you are stressed, even if you just need to vent to someone in a safe space. The important factor is that you should identify an appropriate outlet for your stress.

EXERCISE

Exercise increases the chemicals in our bodies that combat depression and is a proven stress-reliever. Most college campuses offer a recreation facility that is freely available to all students. An exercise routine does not have to be a lengthy and arduous process. In fact, there will be recreation staff available to you to demonstrate the machines that are provided and to establish a basic, healthy exercise routine. Weight training, aerobic training, yoga, and dancing are some types of exercise that you can work on at the fitness gym or your campus' recreation center. If would prefer not to use the equipment at the fitness gym, try going for a run, or do some bodyweight exercises in your dorm room. Stress can create tension in our bodies and exercise creates an outlet for this tension. Make time to be active, especially during highly stressful times.

Outdoor Relaxation

Another method for reducing stress is to spend some time outdoors. Many times, just creating some time to breathe fresh air while you are stressed can positively impact your perspective. There are several ways to incorporate more time outdoors while you are a college student. You can explore the area surrounding your campus by walking. Study outside in the shade when it is warm outside. Take a longer route to your next class if you have enough time. Order take-out food to carry out and eat it at a table or bench outside on your campus. Search the internet or area guidebooks for local hiking trails or swimming holes near your campus. While you are outside, you might be less likely to obsess over a certain issue that has created stress for you. Embrace the change in scenery and think of some strategies that might help the situation that has been stressful.

Personal Time

Because college is an environment of interaction, sometimes stress can be reduced by limiting social contact to allow some personal time. This does not mean that it would be reasonable to stay in your room for days, but there are ways to incorporate alone time in your day. As a student with ASD, you may find that the constant social atmosphere of college can be exhausting. Taking some time alone to refocus and re-energize can make a difference in the way your attitude and behaviors are expressed when you are in social settings. One option to find time to fit in some personal relaxation is to schedule an hour or longer before bed to read, play video games, go for a walk, watch a movie, or learn more about a special non-academic interest. This is a good way to take your mind off the academic and social demands of college. Stress can occur as a result of being tired, and for some students with ASD, social demands can create an exhaustion that can be cured by a little personal alone time.

Make sure that personal time does not detract from your academic progress, however. Keep in mind that you need to have your homework prepared at the end of each day for the upcoming classes. You are at college to learn, so take advantage of the academic opportunities that are presented to you. You can, though, take breaks to make your studying more effective, and also reduce some stress.

Avoiding Procrastination

Any college student will attest to the appeal of procrastination. They will also tell you how detrimental it can be. Procrastination, or putting off an important task until a later time, occurs for many reasons during college. Sometimes procrastination is inevitable based on where the task stands on your list of priorities, but other times situations occur that make procrastination optional. For example, if you have a paper due on a Wednesday that you have not begun, and you still agree to go out with a friend on Monday night, then you are pushing your academic work to a later time. While this can be a minor distraction for some, unless you are prepared to adjust your schedule to fit more work time in before your paper is due, then procrastination can be a catalyst for stress.

To avoid procrastination, try to schedule your tasks and leave a little room for flexibility. Be aware of deadlines and appointment times by using a visual calendar that you will see every day. If you use a cell phone, set an alert to remind you of these dates. Procrastination is much more likely when you have not planned very well. Understand that procrastination will happen at some point during college, and it is not a rare part of college life for most students, but it can be a trigger for stress. Recognize your priorities and keep them in mind. If you miss a social activity so you can study for an exam an extra day, then you will know that you are prepared for an exam and will be able to reschedule social time.

STRESS REDUCERS

The following suggestions are ways to reduce stress. Tick the boxes next to the things that you think could help you reduce the stress in your life at college.

☐ Get out of bed 15 minutes early to avoid potential morning difficulties.

☐ Prepare for your day the evening before. Locate all the things you will need for the next day and put them on a table near your door, pick out your clothing for the next day, etc.

☐ Don't rely on your memory. Write everything down.

☐ Don't do anything that you will have to lie about later.

☐ Be prepared to wait. Not everyone is on your timing.

☐ Maintain good communication. Check email and voice mail so you don't miss anything. Respond to people when they communicate with you to maintain a good relationship.

☐ Don't procrastinate. Whatever you can do tomorrow, you can do today. Don't wait until the last minute for anything because it does NOT help you produce better work. NOBODY is better under pressure.

☐ Plan ahead. Don't wait until you are out of something to restock.

☐ Allow 15 minutes of extra time to get where you need to be.

☐ Always set a contingency plan in case something doesn't go as planned.

☐ Relax your standards. People, papers and projects don't have to be perfect.

☐ Use your energy on good things. Think about the positive things in life instead of the negative.

☐ Ask directions. Take a few minutes to repeat what has been asked of you to make sure you understand.

☐ Say "no" when you should. Recognize that you can't do everything for everyone, so set limits.

☐ Make friends with "low-maintenance" people. Don't create relationships with people who create stress.

☐ Create order in your life. If things feel chaotic in your physical environment, your emotional environment will feel chaotic as well.

☐ Get enough sleep. Your sleep time is how your body recovers from day-to-day stressors.

☐ BREATHE! When you feel stress, stop and breathe deeply.

☐ Write your thoughts, stressors, and fears down in a personal journal. This will get them out of your head.

☐ Talk it out with someone you trust.

☐ Exercise or do yoga. Physical activity releases hormones into your body and brain that will naturally relax you.

☐ Practice. Practice. Practice. The more prepared you are for something, the less stressful it will be.

☐ Change your environment. If you are feeling stressed, change your posture, seat, room, go outside, etc.

☐ Do something for you every single day.

☐ Focus on understanding instead of being understood; on hearing instead of being heard; on loving instead of being loved. You are only in control of you.

☐ Become more flexible with your schedule.

☐ Try new things.

☐ Eliminate destructive self-talk—compliment yourself.

☐ Manage the little things and the big things will take care of themselves.

☐ Allow yourself some reflection time every single day.

☐ Do your least favorite tasks early in the day so you don't have to think about them all day long.

What are some other things that you have found helpful in reducing stress in your life?

_____

_____

_____

_____

_____

_____

_____

_____

FOCUSED COPING STRATEGIES

There are some strategies that can be particularly helpful during times of building stress. These techniques have been identified as specific techniques that people with ASD have used to manage their emotional response to stress.

ISOLATED MUSCLE CONTROL

People with ASD are often able to focus on the details of things rather than seeing the big picture (Attwood 2006). This makes the technique known as isolated muscle control an easy thing for people to do. To use this technique to reduce your stress level, imagine your body in three sections. The first section would include all the muscles in your head, neck, shoulders, and upper back, the second section would include the muscles in your lower back, chest, abdomen, and buttocks, and lower back, and the final section would be the muscles of your extremities.

To use this technique, begin with your first section and isolate each muscle group. Visualize what the muscles look like individually as well as how they connect to the next muscle. Contract and relax each muscle in a rhythmic pattern. Begin at the top of your forehead and move each muscle group in an isolated fashion all the way down to your upper back. After you have contracted and relaxed each muscle in the top section of our body, move to your core. Complete the same process for each muscle in your chest, abdomen, buttocks and lower back. Finally, complete this same process in your extremities starting with your shoulders, moving to your fingertips, then your upper thighs, moving to the muscles of your toes. This process is a way to push the stress out of your muscles from your head to your toes.

DEEP BREATHING TECHNIQUES

The first thing that happens for many people when they begin to feel stress is that their breathing becomes shallow and labored. This inhibits the oxygen that gets to the brain. Through using deep breathing techniques (Freedman 2010), the amount of oxygen in your blood stream will increase. This will allow your brain to tell your body that you are in a relaxed setting that is free from stress. Your whole body will be able to relax with the increased flow of oxygen to your brain. The increased oxygen will also lower your heart rate, lower your blood pressure, relieve any stress headaches, and improve sleep as well as many other things.

To practice this stress-relieving technique, find a quiet location and practice the following pattern:

- Allow yourself to be free of distractions for at least ten minutes.
- Inhale for six seconds.
- Hold your breath for a count of 18.
- Exhale for 12 seconds.
- Repeat at least ten times.

GUIDED VISUALIZATION

The final technique that has proven to be successful for students with ASD is guided visualization (Kasal 2013). This technique involves using the strong memory that students with ASD typically possess. This involves identifying a location from the past that has been very relaxing. It could be a place you visited with your family, your childhood bedroom, or a place you only imagine. This is a technique that you will need help to develop.

If this is a technique you think you will employ during stressful times, connect with a life coach or someone who can assist you to help guide your visualization prior to the onset of any major stress. During this time, you should identify the location and tell the person why that location is relaxing for you. To be prepared for this technique, you should know that your life coach will help you develop your visualization further through questioning. The questions you will be asked will be about what you imagine you are experiencing through all your senses.

The process of this technique is as follows:

- Find a quiet place with your life coach or someone who can assist you and close your eyes.

- Identify and describe your location that is relaxing to you.

- Describe why it is a relaxing place.

- Be prepared to answer these questions from your life coach and give descriptive answers:

  ○ What do you see? (This might be sunshine through the trees, stars in the night sky, computer parts, seagulls flying…)

  ○ What do you hear? (This might be birds chirping, silence, wind through the leaves, cows mooing, waves crashing on the shore…)

  ○ What do you smell? (This might be cookies baking, soap, salty air, fresh cut grass…)

  ○ What do you feel? (This might be wind blowing on your skin, a soft blanket, sand on your feet, water on your legs…)

  ○ What do you taste? (This might be the saltiness of the water, honeysuckle, Mom's cookies, peanut butter…)

The more descriptive you can be with your answers, the better this technique will work. As you are describing what you imagine in your vision, your life coach will write the descriptions for you. After the guided visualization is over, your life coach will give you the descriptors you have identified. You can either use these descriptors in the existing form or to draw a picture of your relaxation space. Depending on your own preference, you can revisit this space when you start to become anxious. For the first few times, you may need to rely on your life coach or a friend to ask you the questions again, but after you become comfortable with this process, you will be able to find a quiet place, close your eyes, and take yourself to your imagined relaxation space any time you need to. With practice, you should automatically be able to revisit the experiences of each sense.

LESSON 4: KNOW YOUR RESOURCES

There may be times when your stress level is too high for you to be able to manage on your own. Luckily, there are a plethora of resources available to you on a college campus. These resources do not exist only in one location for a reason. You may experience a stressful situation anywhere on campus and may need some assistance quickly. To help you identify your potential support people across campus, fill out this information and use it to develop your stress management plan. It would be helpful to identify one person who can be your emergency contact in your time of extreme stress. Save this person's contact in your cell number under the contact ICE (in case of emergency).

Life coach contact information: _____

Peer mentor contact information: _____

Counseling Center point person: _____

Contact information: _____

Dean of Students point person: _____

Contact information: _____

Major department point person: _____

Contact information: _____

Identified friend who understands: _____

Contact information: _____

Family support person contact: _____

BACK TO BASICS

Consider these questions as you prepare to rate yourself on the BASICS of stress management.

B	**Behavior**	What are you doing to actively manage your emotions? Are you managing your own needs daily? Are you following a good sleep schedule? Are you completing personal hygiene tasks daily? Do you have a stress management plan developed? Are you aware of your hot spots and cooling methods?
A	**Academics**	Are you going to class with all your materials daily? Do you have all your supplies for classes? Are you studying each day? Are you keeping up with everything? Do you feel in control of your requirements?
S	**Self-care**	Are you getting enough sleep? Are you eating healthily? Are you planning for your self-care activities? Are you keeping your space clean? What are you doing to make sure you are managing your stress level?
I	**Interaction**	Are you checking in with your support team? Are you planning time for social activities? Are you actively engaged in classes? Are you monitoring your interactions for appropriateness? Have you been offensive or rude to anyone?
C	**Community**	Do you feel like you belong? Are you asking for help when needed? Have you met anyone new? Do you know the names of any classmates? Are you involved in anything socially?
S	**Self-monitoring**	Are you taking care of your own needs? Are you accepting critical feedback? Are you managing your frustration level? Are you willing to see the perspectives of others? Are you advocating for yourself?

BACK TO BASICS: RATE YOURSELF

Take some time to evaluate yourself honestly on the BASICS. Think about what you have learned previously as well as what you have learned about stress management.

B	**Behavior** 1 2 3	**Comments**
A	**Academics** 1 2 3	**Comments**
S	**Self-care** 1 2 3	**Comments**
I	**Interaction** 1 2 3	**Comments**
C	**Community** 1 2 3	**Comments**
S	**Self-monitoring** 1 2 3	**Comments**

GOALS

Personal:

Academic:

Social:

Chapter 7

PERSONAL RESPONSIBILITY IN ACADEMICS

As a college student, consider yourself to be employed on a full-time basis. Your full-time job is that of a college student. As with any full-time job, plan on contributing no less than 40 hours of work per week to be the most successful you can be.

TOOLS FOR SUCCESS

- Attendance
- Out-of-class assignments
- Group work
  - Group work players
- Study habits
  - Study habit tips
- Major/work/career
  - Choosing an academic major
  - Career preparation

INTRODUCTION

One of the major differences between high school and college is the shift in responsibility for academic success. In high school, students are required to go to all classes. High school teachers often allow extensions for assignments, provide study guides that mimic the actual tests, and give very detailed expectations for out-of-class assignments. By its nature, college is designed to enhance skills in students beyond academic achievement.

The shift away from parents and teachers holding the majority of responsibility for a student's academic development to the student holding that responsibility is a key element of the transition from high school to college. Students' success is dependent on their ability to personally monitor attendance, out-of-class reading and assignments, group work, and study time. By understanding the role students have in their own academic success, students can realize their own potential and take responsibility for their own success.

LESSON 1: ATTENDANCE

The first year of college is, for many students, the first time of feeling a sense of freedom and autonomy from parents. In many ways, this is an exciting time for students. No one is reminding you when to go to bed or that you have an exam on a certain day. Your parents are not around to wake you up in the morning before school or to make you do your homework before playing video games. Attendance, in this respect, is a personal responsibility that you must monitor. Students with ASD can especially benefit from regular attendance to each of their classes as this allows for increased familiarity and daily structure.

One of the most common reasons students struggle in college is poor attendance. The correlation between attendance and higher grades stands; the more you attend a class, the better your grade will be. Be careful not to misuse the independence you have earned by going to college. There will be days when you are tired. You might feel like you already know the subject your professor is covering a certain day in class. You may forget to set an alarm and wake up a little late. Try to make it to class anyway. Do not take your education for granted. You are paying for this education, so get the most out of it that you possibly can. Even if you think you know everything about a subject, this does not stand as an excuse or reason to miss class. Going to class is the easiest way to ensure you maximize your academic potential for each class.

For every course you take, you will want to note the attendance policy on the syllabus. If it is not described in the syllabus provided, then ask your professor what his or her expectations are regarding attendance. You will want to know when you will need to provide a note and the number of excused absences allowed. Highlight or underline the attendance policy for each class. Make a note of the attendance policy for each class in your planner. Then, if you must miss a class, keep track of your absences by marking both your syllabus and your planner. Likewise, many courses will note a tardiness policy. Monitor this as well. Some professors might have a policy which states that a student will not be allowed to enter the classroom if he or she is more than 15 minutes late. Be aware of these policies for each class and monitor your absences and tardiness.

Keep in mind that there are some occasions which warrant an absence. If you are sick, have an appointment that could not be scheduled outside of class time, have a death in your family, or experience unexpected car trouble, then these are some reasons you may miss a class. It is essential, however, at these times that you communicate with your professor as soon as possible. You will want to have your professor's contact information in your planner that you carry with you. In most situations, if you communicate before a missed class rather than after, professors will be lenient. Feeling tired, lack of sleep, a headache, forgetfulness, and missed alarms will not count as a valid reason to miss class.

You will want to ensure that you gain access to the material covered in the class you have missed. Ask a classmate if you can copy his or her notes from that class. This is a good way for you, as a student with ASD, to practice social skills. The context of the conversation is a little more predictable than an average small talk conversation. Be polite when asking to copy notes, and realize that the student has the right to deny your request. Your professor might also send a link to any presentations that were given on that day if you have a valid reason for missing class. The important thing to remember is that you are responsible for the material that is provided in every class regardless of your absence. Read and study the chapter in the text and find access to notes from the day you must miss.

It is also important to remember to check your university email for any time or location changes. For some students with ASD, these unexpected changes can be stressful. If, however, you check your email each morning before your classes, you can often prepare yourself for the unfamiliar location or time before you arrive at class and see a note on the door. If class is canceled, then review your notes and enjoy the day off from the class. Remember that your professor has a life outside the college as well, and he or she can experience illness or accidents that prevent attendance at times. Try to remain flexible when this occurs.

Keeping track of your attendance in each class is the key to being a responsible student. It would be very easy to lose track of how many days you have missed class or have been tardy. If you are careful in keeping track of this data, you will be less likely to run the risk of missing too many classes and negatively affecting your grade. An example of an attendance tracker can be something as simple as the following (tick marks indicate classes attended, Xs indicate missed classes).

Table 7.1 Attendance Tracker Example

Class	1	2	3	4	5	6	7	8	9	10	11	12	13	14
Engl. 1010	√	X Overslept	√	√	X Overslept	√	Class canceled	√	√	√	X Overslept			
Biol. 1350	√	X Sick	√	√	√	√	√	√	√	√	√			
Psy 1010	(1/5) √	X Sick	√	Class canceled	(2/5) √	(3/5) √	√	√	√	(4/5) √	√			
UST 1999	√	√	√	X	Class Canceled	√	√	√	√	Class Canceled	X			
Mth 1550	√	√	√	√	X sick	√	Class canceled	√	√	√	√			

Class: Engl. 1010   **Allowed Absences:** 2
Class: Biol. 1350   **Allowed Absences:** 2
Class: Psy 1010   **Allowed Absences:**

Note: The professor will take attendance five times throughout the semester. If I am there all five times he will exempt our lowest test grade.

Class: UST 1999   **Allowed Absences**: 2 excused, 1 unexcused
Note:

Class: Mth 1550   **Allowed Absences**: 3
Note: No late online homework accepted.

ATTENDANCE TRACKER

Complete this table to help you keep track of your attendance in each class.

Class	1	2	3	4	5	6	7	8	9	10	11	12	13	14

Class: _____   **Allowed Absences**: _____
Note: _____

Class: _____   **Allowed Absences**: _____
Note: _____

Class: _____   **Allowed Absences**: _____
Note: _____

Class: _____   **Allowed Absences**: _____
Note: _____

Class: _____   **Allowed Absences**: _____
Note: _____

LESSON 2: OUT-OF-CLASS ASSIGNMENTS

In high school, a significant number of assignments are completed in the classroom. In college, however, most assignments are given to be completed on your own. For students on the spectrum, this transition can be difficult to manage without the proper skills and structure to allow for independent completion. If you can learn to prioritize your assignments, read your texts effectively, and ask for clarification, then you will be able to complete academic assignments. If you have a life coach, work with them to prioritize weekly out-of-class assignments.

First, understand that college coursework is not optional. While you may not be given a quiz or written assignment for each reading in the text that you are asked to complete, realize that the reading is the assignment. It is likely that many courses will have a reading assignment for each class meeting. Read the text *before* going to class so you can follow along with the lecture and have an opportunity to ask questions while they are fresh in your mind. Take notes as you read and highlight important information. Then, after class, while you review, you can add your notes from the reading to the notes from the lecture for a complete guide for studying.

Try to break the reading into smaller mini-assignments. Set goals to read a certain number of pages each day between class meetings. For example, if you have a class meeting on Tuesdays and Thursdays, you will need to read for your Thursday class on Tuesday and Wednesday to be prepared for the next meeting. If you are given a 50-page chapter to read, you can break your reading into two shorter 25-page assignments to complete on Tuesday and Wednesday. The point is not to allow yourself to be overwhelmed by the amount of reading. Think of it as a review. You will prepare yourself for the lecture and exam if you take notes on each. All that you will have to do before an exam is review these notes you have already taken from the text and classroom.

Professors give assignments to provide you with practice for the skills and information you are expected to master as outlined in the course objectives. Every assignment has a purpose. So, complete every assignment you are given and be prepared to hand it in on time. This aspect of college is non-negotiable. Your grade depends on your ability to practice skills and learn new information. Out-of-class assignments give you the opportunity to do so.

The goal of out-of-class assignments is not to confuse you. Ideally, the assignments will help you master information. If you find that you are confused about the instructions for an assignment, ask your professor for clarification. Do not wait until the day the assignment is due to admit that you were unsure of the objective for the work. Talk to your professor before or after class, send an email to your classmates asking for clarification, or see your professor during his or her office hours to ask questions. Do not procrastinate or avoid the assignment because you are not certain of how to complete it. Part of being personally responsible for your academic success in college is being able to independently ask for help and clarification when you need it. "I didn't understand the question" is not an acceptable excuse for a missed or late assignment. Take responsibility and ask questions so you can manage the assignment.

Trying to remember all of your assignments and grades you earned can be a lot to manage in college. Universities often provide online access to track your grades, but these online portals can be difficult to manage as well. There are many apps available through the app store that can help manage this very important task. One app in particular is very inclusive and is very intuitive in design. The app is named Erudio and is available for iPad and iPhone alike (Brown 2013). If you do not have an Apple product, there are versions of these apps available for Android systems as well. If you are more comfortable using a paper-and-pen version of an assignment tracker, you can use a grade book or you can create a paper-based tracking system. The paper-based versions are usable, but do not keep track of your weighted grades for each course. This is something you will need to do on your own. An example of an assignment tracker follows.

Table 7.2 Assignment Tracker Example

Class: ANTH. 3600	Details	Original Due Date	Final Due Date	Completed	Grade
Assign 1	Topic Outline	March 2nd	March 2nd	Yes	92%
Assign 2	Draft 1	March 16th	March 18th	Yes	87%
Quiz 1	In class	Pop quiz		Yes	80%
Quiz 2					
Assign 3					
Assign 4					
Quiz 3	In class	Pop quiz		Yes	100%
Quiz 4					
Assign 5					
Quiz 5					
Mid-Term	In-class test	February 27th	February 27th	Yes	98%
Research Paper	5-page paper	April 23rd	April 25th	no	
Final Exam					
Extra Credit					

ASSIGNMENT TRACKER

Review your syllabi and use the following chart to track your assignments for one of your classes.

Class:	Details	Original Due Date	Final Due Date	Completed	Grade

LESSON 3: GROUP WORK

You will encounter projects in college that have a group work component. Many students feel stress when group work is attached to a grade in the class, but this stress can be increased for students with ASD. Although group work can be difficult to manage at times, it can be beneficial as you learn new material. By working on being flexible with your schedule to accommodate all group members, identifying an element of the project that you feel most confident and competent to complete, managing the social aspect of group work, and practicing presentation skills, students can have a positive experience in groups. This will provide valuable lessons that will help students not only during college but in the workplace as well.

When you meet with your group for the first time, one of the first discussions you will have as a group will be about creating a schedule for subsequent meetings. It is important to remember that all of the students in your group will have different availabilities. As a student with ASD, this kind of scheduling discussion will allow you to practice being flexible. Even if the time that works best for all members of the group is not your first choice of a time to meet, be willing to meet during that time as long as you do not have class or another campus activity. You will need to attend every meeting that your group schedules, so be sure to confirm with your schedule before agreeing to meet at a certain time.

Additionally, since all members of a group will need to contribute to the project or assignment, you will need to identify a couple of aspects of the assignment that you feel the most competent to successfully complete. If you are working on an in-class presentation, you may choose to produce the visual material instead of speak in front of the class, as long as your contributions are equal in terms of effort and quality. Make your group aware of any talent or skill you can bring to the project. If one aspect of the project particularly interests you, then offer to work on that aspect. You may have to compromise and work on a different aspect if that would better serve your group's objective, but this is an opportunity for you to learn something new. The key is to identify elements for which you feel you can produce adequate work that will contribute to the group project. With that said, however, also keep in mind that group work can sometimes be difficult to distribute evenly, so monitor your effort and avoid doing all the legwork for the project.

To navigate the social aspect of a group meeting, try to develop some strategies for effectively speaking with your group. If you have a life coach, you could work with them on this. A positive element of group work for a class is the common theme. All members have the same objective which is to produce a project, presentation, or assignment that earns an acceptable grade. You will not need to become best friends with the members of your group. Your conversations will probably be limited to the content of the course and, occasionally, small talk. Practice your small talk skills and, if necessary, develop a script that you can use as a guide for group conversations, working with your life coach if you have one. You may also consider sharing with the group the ways in which ASD can affect your interaction within a group, especially for those projects likely to take place over the duration of an entire semester.

GROUP WORK PLAYERS

As you progress through your college courses, you will inevitably be assigned a group project. This process is quite challenging, but will give you some insight into how you may work as a member of a team later in your career. If you think of each group member as an actor playing a role, this may be more manageable for you. Each group has a cast of characters that work together to accomplish a similar goal.

THE LEAD

This character is the leader of the group. He or she directs the work, sets timelines, follows up with each cast member, communicates the plan, and ensures completion of the project.

THE TASKMASTER

This character is the person who keeps every other member on task until the goal is met. He or she may control each meeting time, reminding every member to stay focused on the goal and not get off track in their communications or work.

THE RESEARCHER

This character does a lot of the behind-the-scenes work. He or she may look up articles, find resources, develop ideas for the group, or read through the details of the project repeatedly to make sure the group stays on target.

THE WRITER

This character is a strong writer who usually excels in the area of written/visual presentations. He or she may collect every other member's work and combine it into a cohesive presentation of ideas.

THE SPEAKER

This character is a person who is not afraid of public speaking. He or she may be the one the group recognizes as the best person to present the accomplishments of the group to the class. The public speaking skills of this person may be to the group's advantage for the final product.

Which character are you best qualified for? What strengths make you the best person for this role?

_____

_____

_____

_____

LESSON 4: STUDY HABITS

As adults, students will need to monitor their own study time, set goals for their academic success, learn to monitor their effort and take necessary breaks, and create a realistic weekly academic plan. These elements of college life are essential when you consider all of the other factors that can take attention away from the academic goal. Taking responsibility for studying habits in college is especially important to students on the spectrum during the transition to college.

Monitoring study time is one of the most essential skills you will learn as a college student. You will need to create a study plan that includes hours of studying, classroom times, break times, and extra-curricular activities. All students experience this demand in different ways, but for students with ASD, it is imperative that you adhere to some set schedule that you can use to guide your study habits during college. One of the easiest ways to monitor study time in college is to divide work into smaller and less time-consuming portions so that you can complete a task, take a short break, and move on to complete another task on your list of study goals. Remember to take breaks and refocus. It is unrealistic to set aside four straight hours of studying one subject without a break in subject or assignment. If you have a life coach, you can work with them during the early part of each semester to develop habits to increase your effectiveness while studying. Review your planning method and become confident in your ability to monitor your study time wisely.

Students with ASD can have difficulty with monitoring the time needed and spent on topics. They may get lost in time spent on topics, often spending hours on something that should take only minutes. This can cause extreme frustration for students when trying to explain why something doesn't get completed. There are apps available to help manage this time well. Time Timer is one such app that will help you manage your time responsibly. This app takes the place of a loud timer that goes off when your time has expired. It allows you to see the time as it is elapsing, and shows what time is left before you are to move on with the next task. This will allow you to use your time effectively while studying for multiple courses at once. In addition, you can use this timer to limit your break time. Students with ASD can also get consumed by their interest areas during study breaks, and the 15-minute break can easily become three hours.

STUDY HABIT TIPS

- Go to class. Never skip unless you absolutely have to. Seriously. Go to class.

- Create a study plan for your week—especially if you have a test or paper for which you need to prepare.

- Have all of your materials ready when you begin.

- Minimize distractions.

- Study in a well-lit space.

- Keep some water nearby.

- Get plenty of sleep. This is huge. It can make all the difference on exam day.

- Take breaks. Use your digital reminder to set up increments for studying and taking short breaks.

- Alternate between subjects.

- Retype your notes.

- Create outlines for papers and projects, and then complete each smaller task to complete the project.

- Use your campus resources (Writing Center, Center for Advisement and Student Success, and the Disability Resource Center).

- Meet regularly with your academic coach if you have one.

- Choose a study space outside your bedroom. Don't study on your bed. You associate your bed with sleep.

- Go to the library if you prefer a quiet space. Coffee shops are great if you prefer a steady flow. Just avoid places that create distractions. Be honest with yourself—if you can't concentrate when people are chatting, find some space to study alone.

- Make realistic plans for mid-term week and final exam week.

- Always review your notes after class—don't wait until the night before an exam.

- Draw pictures, speak out loud, record the lecture and listen to it at the gym, use flashcards. Be creative! It doesn't have to be pretty in the process as long as the outcome is consistently successful.

- Take advantage of your professor's office hours. They're there to help.

- Turn your cell phone off or at least silence it. You are studying. Disconnect from Facebook, Pinterest, and text messages and calls. Check these things during your breaks.

- Ask for help when you need it. Don't wait until it's too late.

- Don't rely on just your lecture notes. Just because your professor doesn't go over it in class doesn't mean you won't be tested on it.

LESSON 5: MAJOR/WORK/CAREER

For some students, knowing what kind of career they want to have when they are "grown-ups" is a decision they were prepared to make with certainty when choosing a college major. Other students, however, can have difficulty ensuring that the academic major they have chosen to pursue is one that will prepare them for the kind of career they wish to have. Not only that, but some students have no inclination about their future career goals until they are already in college. All of these situations are expected and reasonable for first-year college students. The most vital aspect of choosing a major is to remember that the decision should be based on a student's set of interests. Even if a student does not know exactly what career they are hoping to pursue, his or her interests can lead toward an academic career that is interesting and, therefore, worthwhile. It is important for students to have some ideas that could be considered options for future employment so that students can research the features of many different kinds of positions as they make their decisions.

CHOOSING AN ACADEMIC MAJOR

As a new student in college, you are expected to choose an academic major that will guide the courses you take and, ideally, the path of your career. Choosing a major can be a stressful decision for many students, but if you commit to a major based on your own interests and not those of any other outside influence, the choice can be less intimidating and more fulfilling. After all, your major will determine many of the courses for which you will study and potentially invest in a career. While your parents, siblings, and peers may have suggestions, it is important to remember that you are responsible for your own academic endeavor.

It is not uncommon for students to change to a different major during their time at college. You may be exposed to a course that opens your eyes to a new passion and interest, have a volunteer opportunity that makes you aware of a new future goal, or simply find that you dislike many of the courses required for your current major. Do not be discouraged if you need to change your major. Consult with your life coach, if you have one, and an academic advisor before you do so in order to understand the appropriate steps to take and how to remodel your course schedule. Try to settle into a major by your third year in college. After that, it would become difficult to take all of the classes you will need in order to graduate in a timely manner. However, time and tuition money are small matters compared to your happiness when you leave college, so if you must change your major in order to follow a passion after college, go ahead and work with the Counseling Center on your campus to find alternatives and consider changing your major. Also, be open to having more than one major. This is especially important for students who choose to study liberal arts degrees that might pair easily with another academic focus. For example, if you are studying English or History and have a dream to pursue a graduate law degree, you might consider adding a second major or a minor with a focus in Political Science or Criminal Justice. Once you choose a major that works well for you, the next step is ensuring that you complete all requirements for that degree.

After you have chosen a major, it is imperative that you meet with your advisor in the academic department. You will need to develop a plan for each semester that enables you to take all of the courses you will need to complete the degree. Many colleges require students to meet with an academic advisor at least once a semester to help students stay on track. Your advisor knows the course requirements for your major and he or she can be incredibly valuable during your time at college. If you have questions about your course plans, are thinking about adding a major or minor, or need to discuss post-college plans with someone in the field, your advisor is a great resource for you. Take advantage of every opportunity you have to learn from someone in your field, and remember that you advisor is there to advise you about the courses you need and the academic path that will serve as the foundation of your college experience.

As a student with ASD, you may have difficulty with making this decision and committing to the impact of the decision to choose a major. To help you decide which major may be best for you, visit your Counseling Center or Career Center on campus and take part in the evaluation tools they have for your use. These career interest inventories can give you insight into the question of which major would be the most beneficial for you as an individual based on your interests and personality.

CAREER PREPARATION

Although other people in your life may have sincere intentions when suggesting a major for you, you should take the time to identify those interests that you are willing to pursue. With that said, however, be careful not to focus your career choices on your interest topic alone. While you may be an American Civil War history enthusiast, there are limited jobs available for a narrowly focused subject. It would be difficult to find a career opportunity that is specific to your Civil War interest alone, but you could consider searching for work experience dealing with American History as a general topic instead. You will gain valuable experience and knowledge about the Civil War, but you will also develop a broad range of other skills and knowledge that will make you more marketable when you are considering new positions. It is understandable that you would want to focus intently on your special interest when choosing which career path you want to pursue, but you can benefit from exercising some flexibility as you think about your future. As a student with ASD, your set of strengths and interests will be of tremendous importance as you consider these decisions and practicing patience and flexibility as your begin choosing a major and a career will contribute even further to a successful college experience and career.

Additionally, your first year in college is an appropriate time to start researching the kinds of careers you could pursue given your academic major choice. There are certain elements to every career or job that you should consider while you are doing preliminary research. These elements can include salary range, working conditions, desired level of education, the demand for this particular kind of position, any contacts you may already have, and any contacts you could consider making as you learn more about this career. Keep a list of these jobs as you do your research. It will be helpful as you understand the importance of preparing for the post-college world while you are in college. Take every opportunity to network with professionals who are involved in the career you are pursuing and learn all you can from these first-person accounts of the reality of a career in your interest area.

CAREER EXPLORATION

Researching the basic information about some potential careers can help direct you into the right major choice. Consider your interest area, environmental factors, and salary expectations as you look into some of your potential career choices.

Job/Career	Education Requirements	Interests	Environmental Factors	Salary Expectations

BACK TO BASICS

Consider these questions as you prepare to rate yourself on the BASICS of personal responsibility in academics.

B	**Behavior**	What are you doing to track your progress in your classes? Are you attending class daily? Are you following a good sleep schedule? Are you completing personal hygiene tasks daily? What study habits are you following? What systems have you set up to make sure you are tracking your attendance?
A	**Academics**	Are you going to class with all your materials daily? Do you have all your supplies for classes? Are you studying each day? Are you keeping up with everything? Do you feel in control of your requirements?
S	**Self-care**	Are you getting enough sleep? Are you eating healthily? Are you planning for your self-care activities? What are you doing to stay organized? Are you asking questions when you need clarification?
I	**Interaction**	Are you checking in with your support team? Are you planning time for social activities? Are you actively engaged in classes? Are you monitoring your interactions for appropriateness? Have you been offensive or rude to anyone?
C	**Community**	Do you feel like you belong? Are you asking for help when needed? Have you met anyone new? Do you know the names of any classmates? Are you involved in anything socially?
S	**Self-monitoring**	Are you taking care of your own needs? Are you accepting critical feedback? Are you managing your frustration level? Are you willing to see the perspectives of others? Are you advocating for yourself?

BACK TO BASICS: RATE YOURSELF

Take some time to evaluate yourself honestly on the BASICS. Think about what you have learned previously as well as what you have learned about personal responsibility in academics.

B	**Behavior** 1 2 3	**Comments**
A	**Academics** 1 2 3	**Comments**
S	**Self-care** 1 2 3	**Comments**
I	**Interaction** 1 2 3	**Comments**
C	**Community** 1 2 3	**Comments**
S	**Self-monitoring** 1 2 3	**Comments**

GOALS

Personal:

Academic:

Social:

Chapter 8

CAMPUS SOCIAL LIFE

College is perhaps the most social environment to manage. There are ways to do this successfully even if you struggle with the unwritten social rules.

TOOLS FOR SUCCESS

- The campus social structure
  - College community
- Learning opportunities
  - Marketability
- Balancing it all

INTRODUCTION

As students begin to explore all that campus life has to offer, they will notice that many peers are involved in activities beyond academics. College provides opportunities for students to grow not only as scholars, but as independent members of the greater society as well. To achieve this, universities offer student programs and organizations designed to support students as they pursue interest-driven learning opportunities, increase career marketability, invest in their campus community, and build relationships with peers and mentors in a positive environment. Students with ASD can benefit from the availability of these options as the campus social life can anchor students in an atmosphere conducive to their learning preferences and career aspirations while providing opportunities to develop social skills necessary for post-collegiate life.

LESSON 1: THE CAMPUS SOCIAL STRUCTURE

Throughout your career as a college student, you will be faced with many opportunities to grow personally. The campus social structure is one way in which you can take full advantage of the potential growth. Each college campus differs in what is offered, but the majority of social opportunities fall into five main categories. These categories include:

Major-focused clubs: These often consist of student groups from within the same major who gather weekly to discuss trends and issues in the field. These may also include major-focused Honor Societies.

Leadership development: These opportunities include things such as a Student Government Association and experiences such as LeaderShape. Whether you want to develop leadership skills on a personal level, or have your voice heard on campus as a leader, there are many possibilities available.

Social clubs: "Greek life" is the term often used for fraternities and sororities on campus. There are many potential choices for students who choose to join these groups. Some are more formal and some are more social, but they all value the sense of community that evolves out of being a part of the fraternity or sorority.

Service-oriented clubs: Many clubs begin on campuses out of students' desire to help in some way. Whether you want to help build homes, or create a more sustainable community, you have options in these service types of organizations.

Interest-driven clubs: These clubs are driven purely out of shared interest. Whether you are interested in chess, films, LARPing (Live Action Role Playing), or have a strong tie to a religious organization, there is a club for your interest. If there is not one in existence, as a student, you have the option of starting your own club. There is no excuse for not finding people that share your interest.

COLLEGE COMMUNITY

Just by attending a university, you are part of a community. The community is characterized by the common theme of learning and students have a voice in the manner in which their community is developed and maintained. For students with ASD, this can be an intriguing or anxiety-provoking element of the college environment. With some guidance from support staff, faculty members, and peers, students can learn to embrace this community. As a student on your campus, your peers are often experiencing some of the same new elements that you are experiencing. As you progress through college, you can learn from observing peers, instructors, and service staff members in your campus community.

Learning to value the connections you make with people you meet and spend time with on your campus is one way to ensure that your experience at college is worthwhile. The academic element is often not enough. Even if you receive perfect marks, at some point during your time at college, you will need to call on some member of your campus community for guidance. Become familiar with the kinds of organizations and learning opportunities on your campus and consider joining a group that shares similar interests. Your life coach can work with you to develop a plan for diving into the social atmosphere outside of the classroom.

MAPPING THE SOCIAL WORLD OF YOUR CAMPUS

Use the following chart as a way to brainstorm where you may be willing to take a risk.

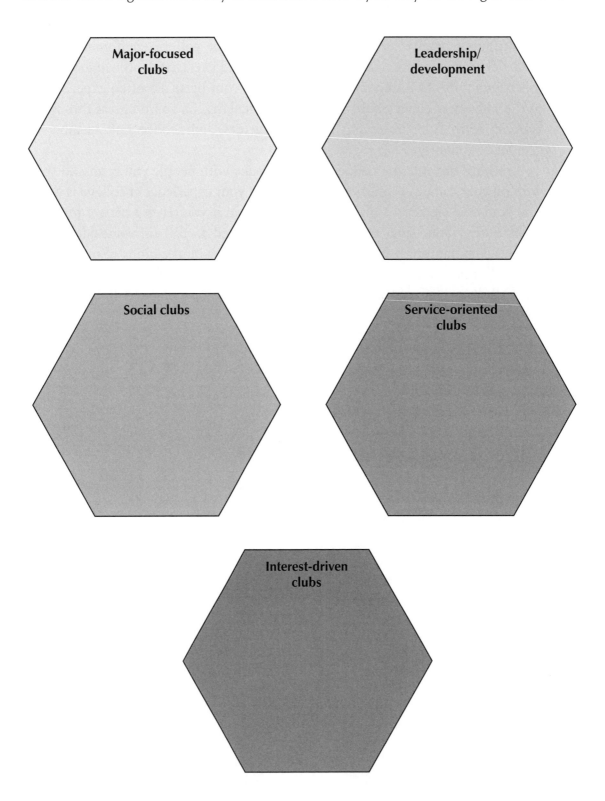

LESSON 2: LEARNING OPPORTUNITIES

As a student, your college administration is invested in creating an environment that can provide support for students pursuing academic degrees. In addition to service-focused departments on campus like those designed to help situate students in internships and build career strategies, colleges also have programs and clubs to help students develop personally. Some programs typically offered to students at campuses include study abroad, leadership development programs, service projects, and student organizations. Most colleges have a plethora of interest-driven student clubs as well. Wherever your interests lie, there is a club out there for you.

MARKETABILITY

Involvement on your campus can not only contribute to your higher education experience, but it will also be a key factor in developing your marketability for your future career. For most students, the motivation to complete a college degree is attached to the desire to obtain a career in a particular field. Employers will be interested in the kinds of activities and organizations that demonstrate your commitment, interests, and leadership. While academic success is of importance, students with ASD can benefit from the increased marketability that is provided by taking advantage of the learning opportunities at college that are interest-driven. You will find that many academic departments on campus have an Honor Society for that particular academic discipline, and these organizations are a great addition to your college experience both while you are studying and after graduation.

Choice 1

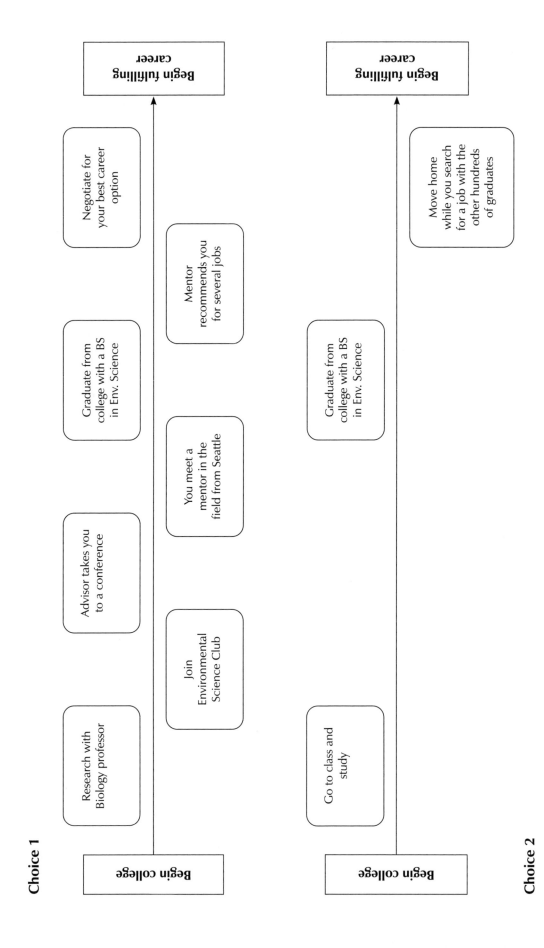

Choice 2

FIGURE 8.1 COLLEGE EXPERIENCE PATHWAYS

COLLEGE EXPERIENCE PATHWAY

The college experience pathway you choose is up to you, but the experience and end result may be very different. Examine each of the previous potential pathways (see Figure 8.1) and choose which direction would be most beneficial for you. Fill in your pathway below and explain your choice.

Begin college

Begin fulfilling career

Why did you outline your pathway as you did?

_____

_____

_____

_____

What connections can help you along your pathway?

_____

_____

_____

_____

LESSON 3: BALANCING IT ALL

For many students, high academic demands and a time-consuming abundance of extra-curricular activities can be exhausting. Successful students find a way to balance academic demands, campus activities, and social life without creating unhealthy habits. While we have stressed the importance of all of these elements in the college experience, these elements will not provide the most benefit if you are constantly stressed about your participation. The first thing you can do to create an effective balancing system for college life is to commit to using a planner to organize your time. In fact, it would be difficult to manage your time if you did not find a way to organize and plan.

In addition, look for ways to do academic work between organization meetings or social events. For example, if you know in advance that you have Student Government Association meetings on Wednesday nights, you can plan to study Wednesday morning before class and before your meeting. Try not to sacrifice any element entirely. Learn to monitor your own time. While you are responsible for your academic success, you also will not want to miss out on all the activities, events, and learning opportunities that college campuses provide. The easiest and most effective way to manage your commitments during college is to develop and commit to some planning system that allows you to recognize important assignment due dates and organization meetings and other campus events in addition to your own social life. Balancing it all is possible if you take the right steps and create a habit of prioritizing and planning according to your priorities.

The unwritten social rules often make taking part in social activities for a person with ASD exhausting. Students often feel like they are actors on stage all the time, always playing a part, hoping they don't forget their lines. The social structure of college and the rules that are part of that may seem elusive and confusing and are difficult at best, but this is something that you can accomplish with some support. The key to managing the difficulties that come along with the growing nature of social relationships is admitting it is difficult and respecting your own personal boundaries.

There is something out there for everyone and there is something on your campus where you will feel like you belong.

BALANCING SOCIAL AND PERSONAL LIFE

When you are balancing your responsibilities as a college student, there are times when these responsibilities might overlap. Some students with ASD have difficulty recognizing some ways to ensure all responsibilities are managed. Academic tasks, personal requirements like recreation and healthy living, and social obligations can often be difficult to manage when they occur all at once. Following the example and prompts below, brainstorm some ways to balance your demands as a college student.

You have a Hist.101 exam on Monday morning. You haven't had much time to yourself during the weekends and you're looking forward to some personal time.

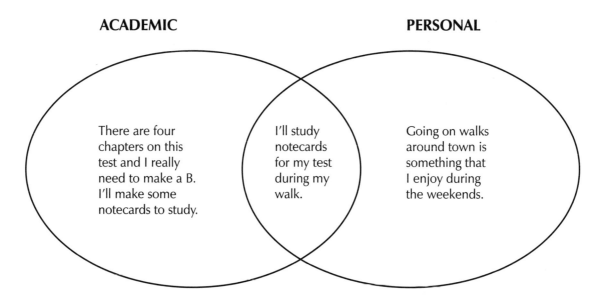

You enjoy playing video games with your friends during your free time, but your laundry is piling up and you haven't washed the dishes you used three days ago.

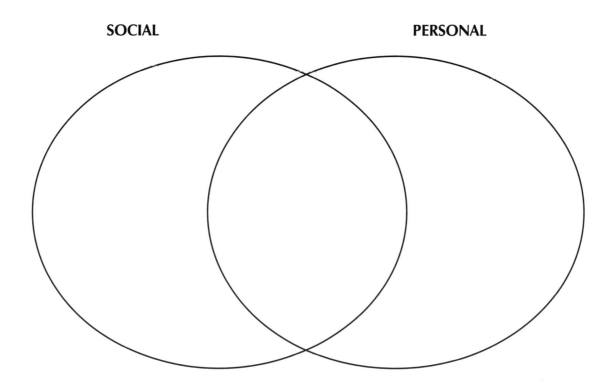

A comic book conference is coming to a nearby city and you have made plans with some friends to attend it throughout the weekend. On Sunday, you are also supposed to meet with your English group to prepare for a presentation you have in class on Monday.

ACADEMIC   **SOCIAL**

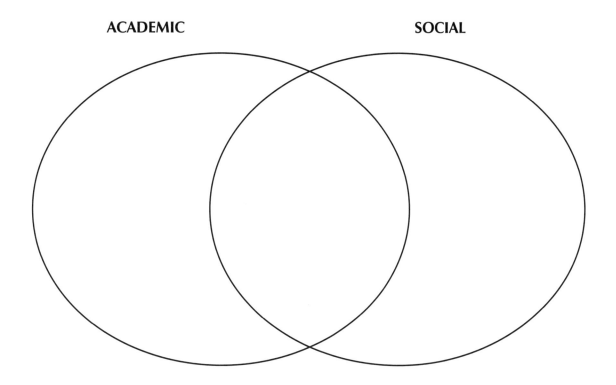

BACK TO BASICS

Consider these questions as you prepare to rate yourself on the BASICS of campus social life.

B	**Behavior**	What are you doing to become socially involved in your campus? Are you managing your own needs daily? Are you following a good sleep schedule? Are you completing personal hygiene tasks daily? Do you know of your major department clubs? Have you visited at least one club?
A	**Academics**	Are you going to class with all your materials daily? Do you have all your supplies for classes? Are you studying each day? Are you keeping up with everything? Do you feel in control of your requirements?
S	**Self-care**	Are you getting enough sleep? Are you eating healthily? Are you planning for your self-care activities? Are you keeping your space clean? What are you doing to take care of yourself after social activities?
I	**Interaction**	Are you checking in with your support team? Are you planning time for social activities? Are you actively engaged in classes? Are you monitoring your interactions for appropriateness? Have you visited at least one club and met at least one new person?
C	**Community**	Do you feel like you belong? Are you asking for help when needed? Have you met anyone new? Do you know the names of any classmates? Are you involved in anything socially?
S	**Self-monitoring**	Are you taking care of your own needs? Are you accepting critical feedback? Are you managing your frustration level? Are you willing to see the perspectives of others? Are you advocating for yourself?

BACK TO BASICS: RATE YOURSELF

Take some time to evaluate yourself honestly on the BASICS. Think about what you have learned previously as well as what you have learned about campus social life.

B	**Behavior** 1 2 3	**Comments**
A	**Academics** 1 2 3	**Comments**
S	**Self-care** 1 2 3	**Comments**
I	**Interaction** 1 2 3	**Comments**
C	**Community** 1 2 3	**Comments**
S	**Self-monitoring** 1 2 3	**Comments**

GOALS

Personal:

Academic:

Social:

Chapter 9

RELATIONSHIPS

There is no scientific formula for managing relationships, but with some understanding of the rules, you can do this too.

TOOLS FOR SUCCESS

- Defining relationships
  - Online relationships
- Recognizing relationship levels
  - The relationship progression pathway
- Sexuality and gender identity
  - Defining of terms
  - Social construction
  - Resources
- Non-optional social compliance
  - Threatening
  - Harassing
  - Stalking

INTRODUCTION

Understanding relationships is an essential component of life on a college campus. Because the campus atmosphere is social by nature, students with ASD will need to develop effective strategies that can help establish and maintain meaningful and healthy relationships. The personal nuances of relationships can be difficult to understand for many students on the spectrum. Yet, while some relationship elements may not come as naturally for students on the spectrum as for others, practicing social skills can make a difference in the way this perceived limitation can be enhanced to affect students' social lives at college.

People with ASD tend to have difficulty in recognizing the social structure of relationships and the skills needed to develop, nurture, and sustain relationships at many levels. This same group of people excels in their systemizing skills (Baron-Cohen 2003). This means that when dealing with relationships, people with ASD tend to try to develop a series of systems that operate on a scientific basis that is rational and unwavering. Unfortunately, people and relationships are fluid, illogical, and unpredictable and follow no existing pattern. This dichotomy makes the idea of relationships a nerve-racking notion for students with ASD. Recognizing and understanding that neurotypical people tend to be driven by emotion instead of logic, feelings instead of systems, will help a student with ASD navigate the bumpy road of relationships. While there is no true algorithm for relationships, there are sets of rules and variances that can be studied.

People with ASD tend to operate in extremes which has been termed as monotropic (Lawson 2005). This can cause some difficulty for developing and maintaining relationships. In the extreme thinking style of ASD, things tend to be black or white, all or nothing. In this style of interpretation, relationships can easily switch from being perfect to being miserable over very small details. This makes the nuances and gray areas very difficult for people with ASD to manage. The difficulty in recognizing other people's views makes the process even more difficult. Understanding these differences can allow people with ASD to develop the logical systems needed to understand and manage the relationships with the important people in their lives.

The many variations in relationships can be defined and the differences in commitment, communication, space, and voice tone among the various levels of relationships can be easily observed. As a student with ASD, if you know what to look for, these signs may become more apparent.

LESSON 1: DEFINING RELATIONSHIPS

In the transition from living at home with parents to being immersed in the college environment with roommates, professors, support service staff, and new friends, students on the spectrum can find understanding these varied relationships to be complicated, confusing, and ultimately a distraction from an otherwise successful academic collegiate career. The first step you will need to embrace is developing a consistent way to define relationships in the various forms in which they are presented. Strangers, acquaintances, friends, boyfriends or girlfriends, and long-term life partner relationships all carry unique elements that define where the relationship is at any given time on the continuum.

Determining the differences between friends and acquaintances or between casual dating partners and a long-term life partner can be challenging for all students. As a student with ASD, the impact of social misunderstandings can exacerbate your difficulty determining where any individual bond exists in a series of progressive levels of personal relationships. It can help to have a general idea of what definition a neurotypical college student might consider appropriate for each of the six general categories of relationships.

1. Stranger: People you do not know personally, or those who you have just met, are considered strangers. Unless you have just met a person, you may not even know his or her name.

2. Acquaintance: An acquaintance is someone you may see occasionally, but you do not know anything personal about this person. He or she may be in some of your classes, say hello to you in passing, and you might know his or her name. Someone with whom you met while working on a group project for a class may be considered an acquaintance.

3. Friend: A friend is someone who knows you personally. You will have each shared details of each other's lives. You may share similar interests and discuss interests outside of class assignments or school-related issues. A friend is someone you trust and in whom you can feel comfortable confiding. There is a reciprocal value to a friendship. He or she is a friend to you, and you must in return be a friend to him or her.

4. Dating: With someone you are dating, time will be shared alone with the other person or in smaller groups, and you may go somewhere planned outside of school. Either you or the other person will have asked the other person to go on a "date" and a positive date will have occurred before you can consider yourself to be dating the other person. Dating is not an exclusive relationship. You may or the other person may also be dating another person.

5. Boyfriend or Girlfriend: A boyfriend or girlfriend is someone you know very well. Personal information is shared between the two of you. This relationship means that you are committed to exclusively being with only the person. At this

level of monogamous relationship, sexual intimacy may be involved, but only if you and the other person feel comfortable with it.

6. Life Partner: A life partner is the person with whom you intend to spend the rest of your life. He or she is someone you can trust completely. You feel comfortable being yourself around this person. This is a supportive relationship. You can count on this person to be there for you and he or she can count on you to be there for him or her. There is typically a physical intimacy involved in this kind of relationship.

ONLINE RELATIONSHIPS

It is not uncommon for college students to utilize online websites for social connection and communication. Websites such as Facebook and Twitter are popular among college students because they allow for virtual social interaction. As a student with ASD, you may be drawn to these kinds of internet-based forms of communication as the social guidelines may be less structured than for in-person interactions. In addition to social media sites like Facebook and Twitter, chat rooms and online dating sites are also forms of personal communication through which students may develop or maintain relationships.

It is important that you understand some of the unspoken guidelines for these kinds of online relationships. Some of the details of the sites may be a bit tricky to decipher. For instance, connecting with people on Facebook is done through requesting to be "friends" with another Facebook user. While the word "friend" is used in the context, this does not mean that every person added on Facebook is a friend who fits the description of being someone who knows you well and supports you. Similarly, if you have a "friend request" from someone on campus, it may be just a way to communicate, but may not mean you will be spending time with this person. It may be a good idea to remember that for social media sites like Twitter and Facebook, you can choose to only become "friends" or "followers" of those people with whom you have an in-person relationship.

Online chat rooms and dating websites are also forms of online relationships. Because there is no need for interpreting facial expression or tone of voice when engaging in an online form of communication, students with ASD may be drawn to online relationships. Valuable relationships can be built through chat rooms and dating websites, but there are some areas where you should be cautious if you are interested in pursuing this kind of interaction.

Keep the following tips in mind if you do engage in social media, online chat rooms or dating sites.

- Never give out personal information, for example:

    ◦ full name

    ◦ address

    ◦ social security number

    ◦ debit/credit card information.

- The terms "friends" and "followers" do not automatically have the same connotation as with in-person relationships and friends.

- If you are preparing to meet someone you met online in person, always choose to meet in a public space.

- Monitor the amount of time you spend engaging in these online options. Do not let your time communicating online interfere with your campus social life or academic success.

- If you feel uncomfortable with someone you are communicating with online, trust your instincts and stop communication.

- People are not always who they say they are online; be careful and ask questions if you are unsure of the validity of someone's online identification.

LESSON 2: RECOGNIZING RELATIONSHIP LEVELS

While there is no true scientific approach for relationships that follow a logical direction to problem solving, there are cues to look for that can tell you which level of relationship you are currently in with any given person. Just as relationships are fluid, so, too, are the levels. Being a stranger to someone one day and becoming an acquaintance the next is possible just as it is possible to be in dating relationships with someone one day and move backwards into being friends the next day.

THE RELATIONSHIP PROGRESSION PATHWAY

In the relationships progression pathway, the arrows represent the work that is being done at each stage. Being committed to actively learning about a person, setting ground rules, and respecting the person as an individual are all things you must be willing to do to move between the stages of relationships. For example, if you would like to learn more about a person who sits in the front of one of your classes, there are steps you can take to work towards the next level of relationship with that person. You can smile at the person, sit closer in the classroom, or wave when you see him or her on campus. Just as there are actions you can take to progress relationships, there are also cautions to take within each level, however.

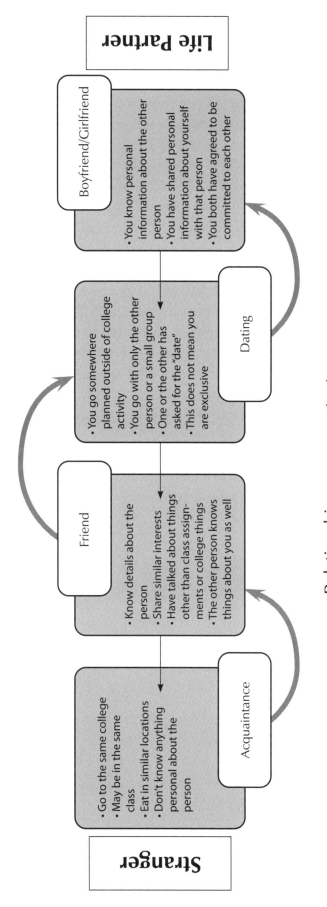

Relationships are a constant process

Figure 9.1 Relationship Progression Pathway

It is also vital to recognize that within each level there are cues to recognizing the intentions of the other person. This is where the relationship puzzle gets interesting. Because people with ASD do not easily recognize these subtle social cues, it will be important to have someone you can talk to about these nuances. This can be a friend, relative, peer mentor, life coach, or anyone you can trust to give you accurate and honest information. It requires a lot of patience and courage for anyone to attempt to enter into a relationship with someone or try to take the relationship to the next level. This task become even more frightening when you struggle with social cues and navigating the constructs developed randomly in society. Although they are subtle, there are rules for relationships and systems that can be established. Use the relationship level progression pathway in the next section to practice this process with someone you trust.

The first step in developing a relationship with someone is to recognize at what level you are with the other person. Use the relationship level algorithm to decipher your starting point. If you determine you would like to move to the next level, use the informational sections and action steps on pages 174–8 as a guide to navigate you through the pathways of relationships. The behaviors represent what the relationship may look like; the signals represent what the other person may be telling you with his/her words or actions; cautions represent what you need to be aware of to protect yourself; and action steps are what you can do to move the relationship to the next level.

To best identify what level of relationship you have with a person, use the following chart to ask yourself some guiding questions. Begin at the top left corner and follow the flow of arrows for your answers. Keep in mind that relationships are not black and white or logical, so some answers may not be clearly defined. Once you identify an approximate starting point of your relationship, you can use the information in the progression pathway to determine your next steps.

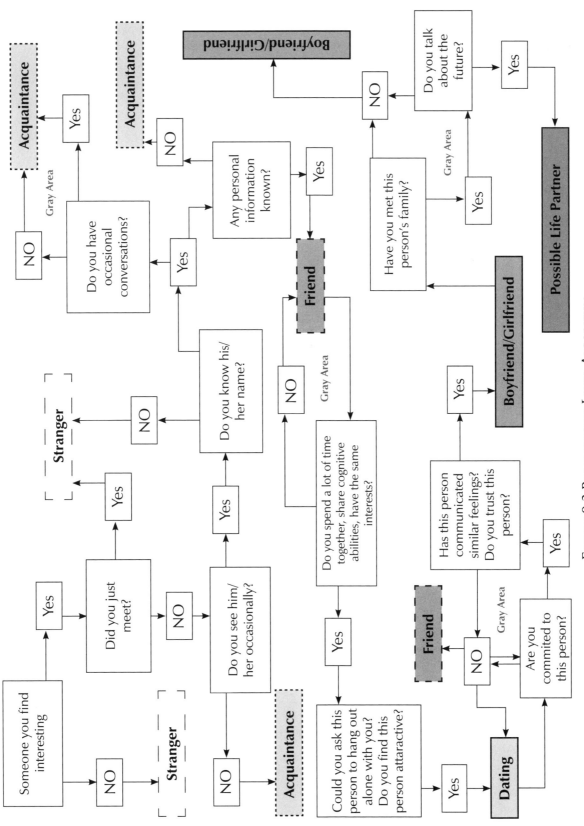

FIGURE 9.2 RELATIONSHIP LEVEL ALGORITHM

STRANGER

Behaviors: This person is someone you have seen before but you have not talked to him or her about anything. You may be in the same class but do not sit by each other or talk about classwork. You have not interacted with this person outside of class.

Signals: If this person wants to get to know you better, they may wave at you, smile at you, or tell you their name. If the person is not interested in getting to know you better, they may look the other way when you approach, not give you their name, or not respond to you when you approach.

Cautions: At this level, you do not know anything about this person. They can use you, steal from you, make fun of you, or hurt you. It is imperative that you move slowly and cautiously at this stage. The other person also does not know you so you must approach with care. This is the level at which many people with ASD get into trouble with the law for stalking or harassing behaviors.

Action Steps	Caution
Wave at the person	Does the person wave back?
Introduce yourself	Does the person tell you his/her name?
Sit next to the person in class	Does the person turn away?
Start a conversation	Does the person respond?

ACQUAINTANCE

Behaviors: This person is someone who may be in your class and says hello to you in passing. S/he might know your name and you may have worked on group projects together. You may have discussed class material in or talked about school.

Signals: If this person wants to get to know you better, s/he may address you by name and introduce you to other people. S/he may ask you about interest areas outside of the class or subject of school, or may invite you to do something with a group of peers. If the person is not interested in getting to know you better, s/he may not address you by name and may not want to talk to you about anything other than class information.

Cautions: At this level, the person may know more about you and may know that you have some struggles with social cues. A person who is not genuine could use that information to get you to do a lot of work in group projects or may try to cheat off you in areas where you are strong academically. The other person also does not know you well, so approach them with care just as in the previous level. Until you know the intentions of the other person, always use action steps in moderation.

Action Steps	Caution
Use the person's name in greeting	Does the person know your name?
Ask how their weekend was	Does the person give you details?
Approach the person when in conversation	Does the person exclude you?
Ask the person what their plans are for lunch	Does the person invite you to join?

FRIEND

Behaviors: This person knows personal details about your life and you have shared interests. You have shared information and know information about the other person as well. Your relationship is trusting and reciprocal. This person may know that you have ASD or not, but accepts you for who you are. You can confide in them and they expect to be able to confide in you as well.

Signals: If the person is interested in moving the relationship to the next level with you, s/he may display flirting behaviors such as sitting closer, show a desire to spend more time with you, touch your arm, or ask if you would like to go to dinner without other people with you. If the person is not interested in allowing the relationship to progress, s/he may not accept your invitation to go somewhere alone, may look at you differently if you attempt to flirt, or may stop talking to you.

Cautions: At this level, you have invested your time and energy into the other person. You may know them more than others around you but could misinterpret the behaviors easily. Use people you trust as a checkpoint to discuss the nuances of the relationship before moving forward. If you do not understand the other person's intentions, you could get your feelings hurt and may lose a friend. At this level, it is easy for a person with ASD to become obsessed with the person and overwhelm them. It is important to value the other person and their needs just as your own. This includes their need for space and privacy. At this level, you can also move backwards in levels if you do not show concern for the other person's needs.

Action Steps	Caution
Attempt to spend more time together.	Does the person avoid this?
Ask the person if s/he has a boy/girlfriend.	Does the person say "yes" or "don't want one"?
Ask the person if s/he is interested in anyone.	Does the person indicate no?
Ask the person to go on a date without others.	Does the person say no?

If the person says "yes," take into account the interests of the other person in deciding on the details of the date, not just your own.

This affirmative response only means yes to one date, not an exclusive relationship. If you want the relationship to become more exclusive, it is important that you focus on the other person's interest and actively discuss those interests with him/her. In addition, it is important that you do not overwhelm the person with emails, phone calls, or text messages. Take things slowly.

DATING

Behaviors: This person is someone with whom you spend a significant amount of time. You know what his/her interests are and show interest in them. You have gone on more than one date with this person which consists of doing something together when not part of a group of other people. The date was a positive experience and you have agreed to spend more time together. This level is not exclusive and you both may still have interests in other people. It is understood that you are not committed solely to each other.

Signals: If this person wants to take your relationship to the next level, they may tell you that the option of dating other people is no longer an interest of theirs. They may ask about spending more time and going on more frequent dates with you. If you talk about another person with this person, they may avert eye contact, turn away from you, or look down. If the person is not interested in progressing the relationship, they may go on less frequent dates with you, may talk about other people with you, or may avoid interactions with you completely.

Cautions: At this level, you may be feeling more invested in this person which could turn into control and obsession if you are not careful. You could misinterpret the other person's intentions and feel more committed to him/her when the feeling is not reciprocated. This could lead to hurt feelings if not approached slowly. Don't avoid this potential level out of fear. This is a good time to set expectations about the relationship. At this level you may unintentionally move back many levels if you do not approach the relationship with care and concern.

Action Steps	Caution
Ask the person on more frequent dates.	Does the person avoid any more dates?
Try to spend more time on dates.	Does the person often say "I have to get home"?
Ask the other person about other people.	Does the person talk about other dates?
Ask the person if s/he want to be exclusive.	Does the person say "no" or avoid the talk?

If the person agrees to date you exclusively, it is important to discuss the expectations of the relationship. At this point, the person probably suspects that you struggle with social cues and managing relationships, so being very honest about this will be helpful. Neurotypical people may have a desire to be loved and needed on a different level and in a different way from people with ASD. Take this into account when entering into a committed relationship.

BOYFRIEND/GIRLFRIEND

Behaviors: This person knows a great deal of personal information about you and you about him or her. You both have agreed to be monogamous in your relationship and have shared the desire to commit to one another exclusively. At this level of relationship, sexual intimacy may be involved but only if both people agree that this is the intention. You share many experiences and spend quantity and quality time with the other person.

Signals: If the other person is interested in making a lifelong commitment to you, s/he will have said "I love you," will talk about your future together, and you will spend time meeting each other's families. The other person may talk about getting married or making a lifelong commitment. If this is not your plan with this person, it is important to tell him/her the truth with concern for the invested emotions. If the person is not interested in moving forward or is expressing a desire to move backwards in the relationship levels, s/he may say things like, "this is moving too fast" or "maybe we should see other people." The person may start avoiding spending time with you or may start being mean to you.

Cautions: At this level, you may feel like you love the other person and want to completely commit to him/her. When people invest emotions into other people, the risk of getting hurt emotionally is much higher, but so is the potential for being very happy. Approach these decisions with caution, but don't avoid them out of fear. Talking about the potential and goals for the relationship is a good approach. At this level you move all the way back to acquaintance level if you do not approach the relationship honestly.

Action Steps	Caution
Tell the person you love him or her.	Does s/he say "I love you" back?
Ask the person about future goals.	Does the person talk about you as part of their future?
Ask the person to meet your family.	Does the person avoid this?
Ask the person how s/he feels about marriage.	Does the person respond in a negative way?

At this level, it is not safe to assume that you both want to engage in sexual intimacy. It is vital that you discuss this and take the other person's needs and views into account as strongly as your own. Your views of lifelong relationships may not be the same. One person may want marriage while the other does not. To avoid emotional strife, discuss the goals of the relationship and needs with each other early, and respect those needs.

LIFE PARTNER:

Behaviors: This person is someone with whom you intend to spend the rest of your life. That could be in a marriage or a lifelong commitment depending on what you both agree to. This is a person you can trust completely and you know that you can make mistakes and that that person will be forgiving of you. This should be a support relationship in which you can rely on the other person to see you as an important aspect of life and s/he can also rely on you for the same thing. There is typically a level of agreed upon sexual intimacy at this level of relationship but that is determined by both parties.

Signals: If the person no longer wants to be in this level of relationship with you, you may see them avoiding you and staying out with friends. If the person has decided to engage in a relationship with someone else, s/he may start being elusive and telling you things that don't make sense. If your intuition is making you uncomfortable with the relationship, ask questions calmly and don't accuse your partner of anything. Be open to understanding what may be causing the strife in the relationship.

Cautions: People with ASD tend to express emotions differently than neurotypical people. This often causes difficulties in long-term relationships. Although it is difficult, it is important to recognize that the other person's needs are just as important as your own, and do whatever you can to meet those needs. Do not engage in anything that makes you feel uncomfortable or that conflicts with your existing morals, but have honest conversations about what you are willing to commit to. Recognize that if a relationship with a life partner ends, it is not always the fault of one person; it may be due to the complications inherent in relationships.

At this level in the relationship progression, there is potential for emotional pain or significant emotional happiness. There is the potential to feel supported and accepted or rejected and hurt. It is imperative to be honest with the other person about your feelings and needs from the beginning. If you do not tell the other person about your struggles, s/he could interpret the difficulty as something s/he is doing wrong. Honesty in the beginning about this will allow for you to work together and to set up a good line of communication.

LESSON 3: SEXUALITY AND GENDER IDENTITY

Just as college can serve as a place to make friends and establish professional contacts, many students begin, or continue, to explore their sexuality and gender identity. The independent atmosphere in which students conduct their social lives, typically outside the scope of parents or teachers, can allow for a unique and empowering development and understanding of individual sexuality. As students on the spectrum continue to increase in number at universities, it becomes pertinent to discuss how an ASD diagnosis may impact students and their understanding of sexuality and gender. It is important to provide some information that could help students recognize how to navigate the complex social world embedded with the often-misunderstood territory of sex.

DEFINING TERMS

Before you can understand how factors like sexuality and gender identity can impact you during your experience at college, there are a few basic terms you will need to become familiar with in order to establish a solid understanding of what it means to be a college student with ASD among more socially versed peers:

Sex: a biological distinction determined primarily by physical anatomy, not society (female or male).

Gender: a social construction used to express masculinity or femininity (woman or man).

Gender Identity: an individual's expression of gender based on personal identity, regardless of biological sex (for example, an individual with biologically male anatomy may have a gender identity by which she expresses herself as a woman).

Sexual Orientation: a term used to identify an individual's sexual attraction to the opposite sex, the same sex, both sexes, or none (heterosexual, homosexual, bisexual, or asexual).

SOCIAL CONSTRUCTION

The idea of gender and sexual identity as social constructs and the notion that concepts of masculinity and femininity must be socially attached to biological sex in order to maintain a societal standard of accepted gender roles is an idea which students with ASD may have difficulty grasping (Lawson 2005). Social construction of gender and sexuality can be described as a culturally defined perception in which society has deemed a particular standard to be "normal" and, therefore, socially accepted and perpetuated.

Consider the manner in which you grew up and developed through adolescence. If you are biologically a female, your bedroom might have been pink when you were a baby before you even had a color preference. You might have been given dolls to play with and perhaps a little pink bike. You will have been expected to be attracted to masculine males. If you are biologically male, your story will probably be a little different. You might have been given toy cars and dinosaurs to play with, a blue bike to ride, and you will have been expected to be attracted to feminine women. There is nothing about being a female that means you must like the color pink or dislike dinosaurs and date men. There is nothing about being a male that means you must be tough, strong, hate the color pink and only date women. The standards for these kinds of gender and sexuality rules are the basis of social construction. So, according to social construction of gender, an individual with a male body must identify with a masculine gender and individuals with a female body must identify with feminine gender identities in order to perpetuate the norms that society has accepted and considered appropriate. Social construction influences many aspects of our lives and depends on the culture in which we live and the values our culture believes to be important.

As a student on the spectrum, you may feel less of an understanding of the social standards of gender and sexuality, and may not feel like social acceptance carries any more weight than self-acceptance. The idea of social rule establishment based on the preference of the majority of the population may not make sense to you. Tying the value of a person or basing your own self-worth on this social construct may make even less sense. Indeed, many students with ASD benefit from this manner of thinking. After all, social standards can influence self-perception in a negative way and, especially in college, getting to know oneself is a large part of developing an autonomous identity.

As you develop as an adult, it is important to understand, however, that these societal rules that suggest what your preferences and personality should mimic are recognized to be "normal" regardless of whether or not this is right or wrong. Students at your college are likely to fit into either the masculine or feminine category and they risk societal judgment should they challenge the standard. Be prepared for these kinds of gender expectations on your campus, but also be aware that you will have support if you find that you do not fall into the stereotypical categories for gender or sexuality.

RESOURCES

Your college years will be filled with personal growth. It would be extremely difficult to graduate from college exactly the same person as you were when you entered. Experiences at college can help you discover new aspects of your strengths, weaknesses, likes, dislikes, interests, passions, and personality.

If you discover that being away from home and living independently has enabled you to think in a way that might be against the social norm, use the resources that are available to you on your campus. If you have questions or would like to learn more about gender norms or sexual orientation, visit the Counseling Center or Women's Center (Palmer 2006) on your campus. These can be great resources for you as you take the steps to understand more about this issue. Lastly, try not to forget that you can consider the Disability Resource Center on your campus to be a safe place to find support.

CONTACTS FOR SEXUALITY OR GENDER-SPECIFIC ISSUES

Fill in this chart so you are aware of the campus resources available for you if you have any questions or concerns with sexuality or gender-specific issues.

DEPARTMENT	CONTACT PERSON	PHONE NUMBER	OFFICE LOCATION

LESSON 4: NON-OPTIONAL SOCIAL COMPLIANCE

Whether you understand the purpose of societal norms or the rules that come out of those norms, there are a few rules that are non-optional. Dr. Jane Thierfeld-Brown refers to these rules as rules of Non-Optional Social Compliance. This simply means that regardless of whether you understand or agree with these rules, you are required to comply with them or face legal ramifications. Some of these rules are directly related to relationships.

The nature of relationships is difficult to manage for people with ASD. Even with the most detailed information provided and all the tools to help you learn to navigate relationships, there may be some difficulties that arise. Unfortunately, some of these relationship difficulties could result in legal issues. While the behavior related to these relationship issues may not be what you intend, if the other person perceives a threat, that is what will be understood to be the truth. Some areas that will be very important for you to pay close attention to are behaviors that could be interpreted as threatening, harassing, or stalking.

THREATENING

As a college student with ASD, you will be faced with many situations throughout your college career that may be frustrating to you, may seem unfair, or may hurt your feelings. These situations may be particularly difficult for you to manage due to particular struggles with emotional regulation and managing your tone of voice. Because students with ASD tend to struggle consistently in these areas, the ability to manage an emotional situation can escalate very quickly, resulting in someone feeling threated by you. Whether you intend to threaten someone or not, the perception of the situation will dictate the response of others.

In a situation where you are feeling an emotional surge, it will be very important for you to recognize that you are getting emotional (angry, upset, sad). In this situation, your first reaction should be to leave the situation and find someone you trust who you can talk to. This person can help you see the situation clearly and help you tailor your response so it is not seen as threatening. Use the following examples to examine inappropriate responses and to brainstorm ways the situation could have resulted in a different interaction if the more socially acceptable behaviors were displayed.

EXAMPLE

Josh is in an introductory English class during his freshman year in college. He gets his first paper back and has earned a grade of a "C" because he did not clearly address the requirements of the assignment. Josh approaches the professor after class and asks him why he didn't make the requirements more clear. The professor reminds Josh that all the requirements are outlined in the class syllabus. At that point, Josh tells the professor it is his job to make sure his students understand the requirements so he is failing at his job and should not receive tenure. Before he knows it, Josh's voice has become very loud and he is standing very close to the professor. Campus police enter the classroom and escort Josh out of the area and report him to Judicial Affairs for threatening a professor.

How could this situation have been resolved in a more socially acceptable way?

_____

_____

_____

_____

_____

_____

_____

_____

_____

_____

EXAMPLE

Bill is working in a group with other classmates on a project. One group member consistently disagrees with what Bill believes to be the true purpose and solution to the project. Bill sees that group member at the grocery store and approaches him to talk about the project. Bill gets upset and stands very close to the other group member. At one point Bill yells, "You are so stupid. How did you even get into college?" Bill continues to yell and get close to the other student because he will not concede to Bill's opinion. Before he is aware of what is happening, the police arrive and escort Bill out of the store. He is charged with threatening behavior and now must go to court to defend his actions.

How could this situation have been resolved in a more socially acceptable way?

_____

_____

_____

_____

_____

_____

_____

_____

_____

In both of these situations, the person with ASD did not intend to cause fear or harm, but the other person involved perceived a level of threat. What parts of the interactions could have been perceived as threatening?

_____

_____

_____

_____

_____

Non-optional Social Compliance Rule: Do not threaten in any way with your voice or your body.

- When interacting with someone who does not agree with you, never raise your voice to the level that can be heard as yelling.

- When interacting with someone in a situation that is volatile, stay in your own personal space.

- NO MEANS NO!

HARASSING

Harassing is another behavior that is directly related to relationships that can be even more difficult for students with ASD to manage. Because it may be difficult for you to read another person's body language, you may not know that they do not want to talk to you, go on a date with you, or take phone calls from you. In addition, if the other person does not know that you have ASD, he or she may interpret your behaviors as weird and scary.

In a situation where you are trying to engage in a relationship with another person, it is imperative that you make your advances gauged on the responses of the other person. You can, again, discuss the situation with a person you trust and ask for guidance about the next steps. You can also establish a set of guidelines for how many emails, phone calls, or text messages would be appropriate, or if it would be appropriate to go to the other person's place of residence.

EXAMPLE

Caleb has been tutoring a female student in Biology class and he is beginning to feel attracted to her. She has given him her email and phone number to schedule tutoring sessions and to communicate and schedule changes. On Friday night, Caleb decides to email her and ask her to go on a date with him. He does not hear back from her that night, so on Saturday, he text messages her and asks her if she received his email. She still does not respond so he text messages her another five times with various questions. Finally, on Sunday morning, Caleb calls her and leaves a voice mail asking why she won't go out with him. He can't let the idea go, so he calls her several more times throughout the day. On Monday, she tells him that she has found another tutor and that he should never call, text, or email her again. That afternoon, he sends a three-page email explaining why he contacted her so many times and just to make sure she got it, he texts her and calls her again.

How could this situation have been resolved in a more socially acceptable way?

_____

_____

_____

_____

_____

_____

_____

_____

_____

_____

EXAMPLE

Christie is in a Chemistry class that she really enjoys. She has communicated with her professor many times and he has talked to her about how good she will be in the field when she graduates. Christie has increased the amount of time she is spending in the professor's office during office hours and has recently been asked to leave so other students can have time with the professor. To make it easier on her professor, Christie searches for his home address and decides to go to his house to talk to him. He has shown interest in her development so she wants to spend more time with him to grow professionally. She goes to his house on a Saturday afternoon but he is not home. She sits on his front porch for several hours until her professor arrives home with his wife and children. When he asks Christie why she is there, she tries to follow him into his home so they can talk further.

How could this situation have been resolved in a more socially acceptable way?

_____

_____

_____

_____

_____

_____

_____

_____

_____

In both of these situations, the student is not intending to harass the other person or threaten them in any way, but it can be perceived that way. How could these interactions have been perceived as harassment?

_____

_____

_____

_____

_____

Non-optional Social Compliance Rule: Do not harass in any way through physical interaction, email, text messaging, or phone calls.

• Never go to a person's residence uninvited.

• Limit the amount of communication sent to a person to three messages until you hear back from the other person. Those three messages should not be on the same day.

• NO MEANS NO!

STALKING

Stalking is a behavior that is even more difficult for students with ASD to manage than the previous two. Because students with ASD have some level of difficulty with communicating effectively, this is a point of anxiety for many. Whether the difficulty is in formulating the message you want to convey verbally or reading another person's body language, both must be considered when approaching a stranger for the first time.

In a situation where you would like to approach someone to talk with them, it is always best to have a script in mind for what you can say. Your support people on campus can help you develop this script for approaching a person to have a conversation. This script can be in your head or on paper, whichever works best for you. There will be times when you see someone you would like to approach, but have not had time to prepare a script. That is when having a general conversation introductory script developed can be very helpful. Although you may not have any malicious intent, but are simply struggling with what to say to someone, again, it is the perception that will matter, not your intention.

EXAMPLE

John is walking up the hill from the dining hall. He is walking alone and notices a girl walking in front of him. She is very attractive to him and she is walking alone too, so he is not as afraid to approach her. He walks behind her thinking about what to say to start a conversation. Should he just say "Hi, I'm John" or should he be more specific and say something like "Hi, I noticed you walking alone and would like to walk with you if you don't mind." Then he thinks that would be too many words so he formulates another approach in his mind where he combines the two with less words… Before he knows it, he is standing in the girl's residence hall right outside her door and she is quickly trying to get her keys in her door while she is looking over her shoulder.

How could this situation have been resolved in a more socially acceptable way?

_____

_____

_____

_____

_____

_____

_____

_____

_____

_____

EXAMPLE

Stephanie is working at an internship at a local business and is very interested in getting to know a co-worker. She feels that this other person has a lot in common with her and she is very intelligent so Stephanie thinks they can have a great conversation as colleagues. Every day Stephanie stands outside in the parking lot near the co-worker's car planning to talk to her. Each day, she get scared and just stands there and watches her get into her car and pull away. After two weeks, Stephanie is called into her supervisor's office where she is told that the co-worker has complained that Stephanie is stalking her and she will now have to leave the internship.

How could this situation have been resolved in a more socially acceptable way?

_____

_____

_____

_____

_____

_____

_____

_____

_____

In both of these situations, the person with ASD was struggling with how to start a conversation, did not read the body language of the other person and displayed stalking behavior although there was no intended malicious behavior. What kinds of body language could the person with ASD have looked for or noticed that would have identified that the other person was uncomfortable?

_____

_____

_____

_____

_____

Non-optional Social Compliance Rule: Do not display behaviors that could be perceived as stalking.

- Never follow a person for more than two minutes without saying something to him or her.

- Never sit and wait for someone near their vehicle, residence, classroom, etc. if you are not at least at the relationship level of friend.

- NO MEANS NO!

CONCLUSION

Relationships are the most difficult and confusing thing to manage for everybody, whether you have ASD or are neurotypical. People are unpredictable and often driven by emotions. This is what makes relationships between people so obscure. While there are not many identified rules of relationships, knowing the few that exist can help you develop and maintain relationships or at least stay out of trouble with the law. There is no formula for developing relationships, but if you are open to learning the process, you will discover the path to follow, so you too can be successful in relationships.

BACK TO BASICS

Consider these questions as you prepare to rate yourself on the BASICS of relationships.

B	**Behavior**	Are you following the pre-set rules for personal space? Have you identified people in your life who are at different levels in the relationship progression? Do you understand the differences between each level? What are you doing to make sure you are not displaying threatening, harassing, or stalking behaviors?
A	**Academics**	Are you discussing opinions appropriately with your peers? Are you making use of your professor's office hours appropriately? Are you maintaining good personal space boundaries?
S	**Self-care**	Are you getting enough sleep? Are you eating healthily? Are you planning for your self-care activities? Do you know your resources for relationship/identity support?
I	**Interaction**	Are you checking in with your support team? Are you planning time for social activities? Are you monitoring your interactions with people? Are you checking your email/blackboard daily?
C	**Community**	Do you feel like you belong? Are you asking for help when needed? Have you met anyone new? Do you know the names of any classmates? Are you involved in anything socially?
S	**Self-monitoring**	Are you managing your time? Are you accepting critical feedback? Are you having a positive or negative impact on people around you? Are you advocating for yourself?

BACK TO BASICS: RATE YOURSELF

Take some time to evaluate yourself honestly on the BASICS. Think about what you have learned previously as well as what you have learned about relationships.

B	**Behavior** 1 2 3	**Comments**
A	**Academics** 1 2 3	**Comments**
S	**Self-care** 1 2 3	**Comments**
I	**Interaction** 1 2 3	**Comments**
C	**Community** 1 2 3	**Comments**
S	**Self- monitoring** 1 2 3	**Comments**

GOALS

Personal:

Academic:

Social:

NEXT STEPS

Students on the autism spectrum experience college through a lens which may, at times, enlighten their perspective, or, at other times, make it a bit foggy. Transitioning to college and navigating through the new social territory while also trying to manage academic coursework can be exhausting. With this guide, you have been given tools for success that can help you manage during transition times in your life. Return to the BASICS when you need a refreshed perspective on the transition process, communication strategies, academic responsibility, relationships, and individual development. Use the resources available to you on your campus or in your community, and don't forget that you are not in this alone.

As a next step, be prepared for more in-depth work exploring the impact of ASD in college. You will learn how your diagnosis can become the catalyst for empowerment and personal growth. Leaning on the concept of self-reflection, the next guide will focus on developing a new view of yourself as a person with ASD.

BACK TO BASICS CHART STUDENT EXAMPLE

B	**Behavior** 1 2 **3**	**Comments** I am starting to become more aware of some of my behaviors. I really like it when people offer me suggestions as long as I am sure what they mean by them. I am still working on identifying areas in which challenges are presented, but I am more aware of areas that I am experiencing growth in.
A	**Academics** 1 **2** 3	**Comments** I am starting to really lean on my support team. I am attending all but my Geology class because it is at 8am and I cannot get out of bed. I still need to complete 2 of the 4 study hours.
S	**Self-care** 1 **2** 3	**Comments** I go to bed every night around 11pm and get up around 8am so I am getting enough sleep. My roommates have been complaining of my messy room so I probably need to clean.
I	**Interaction** **1** 2 3	**Comments** I do not like speaking up in class or checking my email. I would much rather play a video game in my room or listen to music. I am not used to all these people constantly being around me.
C	**Community** 1 **2** 3	**Comments** Sometimes I feel like I am so different but when I am around others in this class I see there are people like me out there. I don't typically like meeting new people but most of us have common interests so that has been really cool.
S	**Self-monitoring** 1 **2** 3	**Comments** I realize now that I could do a better job advocating for myself so that is one of my new goals for the semester. I really am not good at time management but since I started using my phone for reminders, I am getting better.

GUIDED DISCUSSION

In this section, points of discussion and guiding questions are offered for each chapter. This information is intended to be a starting point for conversation and should be built upon based on the needs of the group, class, or individual. These suggestions are proposed to provoke thought about the material, and it is the hope of the authors that each user will build upon these suggestions to make this material useful for each user.

CHAPTER 1: TRANSITION TO COLLEGE

LESSON 1: LIFE SKILLS DEVELOPMENT

DISCUSSION POINTS

When students with ASD transition into college, many of the things that parents have done for them become their responsibilities. This is a difficult thing for any student to plan for, but particularly so if you have to develop your own routine for the first time. Some very important things to think about are the ability to manage your own medication and remember to take that medication, developing the skills necessary to live independently without an adult guiding your daily activities, developing and maintaining healthy eating habits and healthy hygiene schedules, and finally, developing an organizational system to keep all the requirements in order.

GUIDING QUESTIONS

- What are some things that your parents or adults in your lives have done for you?

- What information do you need in the event that you become ill or injured on campus?

- How can you communicate that information to health care providers?

- If you are on prescription medication, what would be the impact of not taking that medication as prescribed?

- How do you currently manage your medication? What reminder systems have you set up to take your medication as prescribed?

- What types of daily activities are you concerned about doing on your own? (Waking yourself up in the morning, keeping your living environment clean, taking showers routinely, budgeting your finances, communicating your own needs…)

- What kind of food allergies or aversions do you need to monitor?

- How do you plan to meet those needs in a healthy way with your meal plan?

- Hygiene is something that quickly gets overlooked among all the other requirements of a college student. Use the Cleanliness Checklist on page 22 to remind yourself of these vital steps to keeping yourself clean and healthy. Are any of the expectations outlined in this checklist unfeasible?

- Students often claim that they never needed an organizational system in high school. That will change very quickly in college because the expectations and amount of information to be processed is much greater. In addition, students must now organize everything on their own. Outline what types of organizational systems you have tried, and share what has worked about each.

LESSON 2: SELF-ADVOCACY

DISCUSSION POINTS

At this stage in your life, it is very important to begin to advocate for yourself and your needs. Sometimes this is difficult because having a conversation with a roommate or a professor may be difficult, but writing a script and practicing with someone could be very helpful. Whether you are communicating your academic needs with professors or developing a roommate contract, you will be responsible for ensuring that your needs are met. You may not have your parents or another educator with you to guide those conversations. Being well prepared for these conversations can make them less stressful and more effective.

GUIDING QUESTIONS

- What are your concerns about sharing space with a roommate?

- What things are important for you in your living situation?

- What things do you want to keep out of your living situation?

- What is your requirement for sleeping (sound, light, times)?

- What types of academic accommodations have you used in the past?

- What academic accommodations do you think you will need to have in college?

- The process of requesting accommodations is very different from how it was in high school. You will be the person responsible for communicating the accommodations you need for equal access. What do you know about the process of requesting and managing accommodations at your college?

- As you are a college student, information about your disability is confidential. The impact of ASD is difficult to mitigate in a college classroom so it may be wise to think about disclosing this information to your professors. What would be the benefit of disclosing this information? What might be the harm in disclosing this information?

- When would you feel like you should disclose information about the impact ASD has on you individually?

- How do you think scripts would be helpful in framing these and other conversations?

LESSON 3: UNDERSTANDING AUTISM SPECTRUM DISORDER

DISCUSSION POINTS

Students often go through school attending meetings where adults and educators talk about what they need in the classroom. Perhaps students do not even get an official diagnosis until late into their school career. Whatever the reason, students often come to college without a strong understanding of ASD, which puts them at a disadvantage. It is imperative that you understand not only ASD in general, but also more specifically how you are impacted individually. The Impact Triad (see pages 33–36) is an identification of the three major areas impacted by ASD: social/emotional issues, flexibility of thought, and communication. These areas can be explored more thoroughly by examining the concept of Theory of Mind which refers to the ability to understand the mental state and perspective of other people. Another concept to increase the level of understanding of ASD is the concept of central coherence. This addresses the need for you to be able to manage everything in life at the same time to form a complete picture. Finally, it is important to recognize that executive functioning skills are impacted on a large scale. This set of skills is vital to be successful in college, but are a significant weakness among college students with ASD. Developing a support system in a proactive way can help you experience a lower level of stress and a higher level of success.

GUIDING QUESTIONS

- What do you know about ASD?
- How does ASD impact you personally?
- What is the impact of ASD on your relationships with other people?

- People with ASD tend to first examine all the details, and then logically link those details to create a larger picture. This makes managing all the details of college life difficult. What types of things do you expect to have to manage daily while at college?

- People with ASD are often impacted in three distinct areas to varying degrees. Which of these areas are impacted the least for you?

- Which of these areas do you need support in developing?

CHAPTER 2: ORGANIZATION IN ACADEMICS

LESSON 1: PLANNING SYSTEMS

DISCUSSION POINTS

Getting and staying organized is one of the most important components to becoming a successful college student. It is no surprise that it can be one of the most challenging tasks for individuals on the autism spectrum. Imagine a file cabinet with file folders full of papers organized neatly and alphabetically. This is what may be taking place in the brain of someone with a good organizational system. It may be valid that you didn't need an organizational system in high school because you were able to remember everything, but that will not be the case in college. While you think you were remembering everything in high school, it is probably more accurate that you had others reminding you to complete tasks, turn in homework, stay focused, etc.

Now imagine that same filing cabinet overflowing with miscellaneous papers in no particular order, files misplaced and buried under other papers. That is what may take place in your brain in college if you do not develop an effective organizational system. It is important to remember that no matter how you organize things you are expected to meet the requirements of the course, and that means understanding the concepts, doing assignments, turning them in on time, and following each professor's instructions. Organization systems are about more than academics. This is a habit that you will use for the rest of your life.

GUIDING QUESTIONS

- What are you currently using to organize your life?

- What keeps you focused?

- How well do you handle change in your routine?

- What are ways you can implement flexibility to your scheduling?

- How much time do you think you should be spending on studying for each class?

- Do you plan day by day, week by week, monthly, or at all?

- How do you remind yourself of tasks that must be completed?

LESSON 2: MANAGING TIME AND ASSIGNMENTS

DISCUSSION POINTS

Once you have established a method for organizing the tasks and requirements in your life, you should also develop a method for managing your time. College students with ASD have expressed that one of the most difficult things to do during the transition to college is to manage independently the amount of time spent on specific tasks. Whether you spend an overabundance of time on one assignment, or get distracted by a special interest area, finding a routine in which you spend an appropriate amount of time on all requirements is vital. An initial step to developing an effective time management system is to access your syllabi for each class through your campus course management system. Evaluate what must be completed throughout the semester and assign a timeline for each piece. This timeline can serve as a skeleton to your semester time management system. Once the timeline is established, set visual reminders or cues through a paper-based or technology-based system to remind you of these timelines.

When students transition to college, it is often the case that all the priorities get mixed in together. When you have five courses with requirements for each, social events, personal time, family events, and recreational activities to manage, it may become difficult to determine which is most important. A prioritized and detailed "To Do" list can help you outline what requirements must be met each week. By placing priority levels on these tasks according to due date and point value, you may be able to evaluate what amount of time should be spent on each task and in which order they should be completed. An added value of this approach is the ability to highlight each task as it is completed. This allows for the rewarding feeling of completion to take place while still being able to read exactly what was accomplished that week.

GUIDING QUESTIONS

- What takes you the most time to complete academically?

- When during the day do you do your best work?

- Do you need breaks throughout the day?

- How long do these breaks usually last?

- How difficult is it for you to refocus after a break?

- What things distract you from what you need to accomplish?

- What do you need from those around you to feel accomplished?

- How do you currently prioritize your requirements (your social life, assignments, meetings, studying)?

- What happens when multiple things are happening at once?

- How do you decide what to work on when you have two papers due on the same day?

- How do you currently decide what is most important on your list?

- How do you build time in for social activities and personal time?

- How do you currently track your completed tasks and the items that still need to be finished?

LESSON 3: SETTING GOALS

DISCUSSION POINTS

Talking about things we would like to accomplish is a good thing to do, but actually setting goals with achievable timelines and writing them down helps students make a commitment to take action. Setting realistic short-term and long-term goals can help you accomplish goals frequently while keeping a goal for the future in view. Reflecting on the accomplishment of goals helps you identify what may be interfering with your success. This will encourage you to become a more self-directed, self-monitoring student. Your goals should be focused around the equally important academic, personal, and social areas to allow for holistic well-being in your life.

GUIDING QUESTIONS

- What is the difference between a short-term goal and a long-term goal?

- What do you hope to achieve with your goals?

- How do you prioritize your goals?

- How realistic are you in being able to set and achieve these goals?

- What is your time frame in accomplishing these goals?

- How can you break your goals down into manageable steps?

- What can you do today that will help you reach your goal?

- How do you keep track of your success?

- Are these goals relevant to success and happiness?

- Are you prepared to follow through with meeting these goals?

CHAPTER 3: COMMUNICATION IN ACADEMICS
LESSON 1: USING A SYLLABUS

GUIDED DISCUSSION

Using effective communication strategies is a skill that is incredibly important in a student's ability to progress through college successfully. Many questions and confusions could arise for students and understanding how to clarify expectations with professors appropriately is the key to success. The first step in understanding expectations is to know how to read the syllabus developed for each course. A syllabus is a detailed outline of course expectations You will have different professors with various styles, but each syllabus will have vital information you will need to know to navigate the semester successfully. Some information you could glean from your syllabi includes, but is not limited to, professor contact information, attendance policies, grading scales, and course schedules.

Many professors keep grades posted and up to date in an online course management software system much like you may have experienced in high school with teachers consistently informing you of your progress. As a responsible student, you should depend only on this method of monitoring. By assessing the weight of grades and course expectations, you should be able to stay up to date on all of your grades at all times. In college it is your responsibility to always know where you stand. If you wait until professors report your grades at mid-terms, it may be too late to make adequate progress to achieve an acceptable grade. By maintaining a clear understanding of your status, you will be able to make responsible decisions about your courseload. Knowing your grade at all times is your responsibility and is the only way to be in control of your academic outcomes.

GUIDING QUESTIONS

- How can a syllabus be useful to you?

- What are some ways you can get in touch with your professor?

- What time does your class start? Where does your class meet?

- Is there an attendance policy for your course?

- Are there any important dates listed (for exams, assignments, no class, projects, or papers)?

- Does this professor use a course management site?

- What does your syllabus say about how your grade will be calculated?

- What does it say about make-up work and late assignments?

- How will you keep up with deadlines for your courses?

- How is your grade calculated for each course?

- What is your grade goal for each class?

- How will you keep track of your grades?

- If someone asked you your grade in a class, at a random time throughout the semester, how would you know what your grade is?

- If you are keeping up with the reading, taking notes, attending class and still struggling, what should you do?

LESSON 3: ACADEMIC COMMUNICATION

DISCUSSION POINTS

Communicating clearly is a difficult but necessary step in your college career. Often, students become confused about expectations and are so uncomfortable with addressing the faculty member, they would rather ignore the problem and allow the grade for the course to suffer. However uncomfortable you are with communicating, your grades depend on your ability to discuss your confusions with professors and to ask for the help and guidance you may need. Some things to keep in mind are the preference for how your professor chooses to be addressed (Dr., Mr., Professor), scheduled office hours of your professors, and the preferred method of communication. Regardless of how your professor prefers to communicate with students, you must always communicate clearly and respectfully. Finally, realize that your body language in class and in meetings communicates volumes about you. Regardless of the intention behind how you carry yourself, the perception your professor develops about how you present yourself will weigh heavily on your interactions.

GUIDING QUESTIONS

- What can you gain from talking to a professor?

- Why is checking your email frequently so important?

- How do you determine whether or not to read an email?

- How should you construct an email or email response to a professor?

- If you are going to miss class, how should you communicate that with your professor?

- What conversations should take place in a classroom as opposed to a confidential setting?

- How much time should you take to talk with a professor during office hours?

CHAPTER 4: ORGANIZATION IN LIFE

LESSON 1: MEDICAL HEALTH

DISCUSSION POINTS

As students with ASD transition into college, unfortunately, many young adults decide that they no longer want to take or forget to take the medication they have been prescribed. This has frequently had a negative impact on students through the transition process. The transition to college is difficult enough without forcing your body and mind to go through a medication level change as well. Although you may feel that you can manage without the medication you have been told to take, this is not the time to make these changes on your own. Any change to medication dosage should be monitored by a medical professional to avoid any potential negative side effects.

GUIDING QUESTIONS

- What medications do you take daily?

- What are you prescribed these medication for?

- What would be the impact of not taking the medication as prescribed?

- Medication as prescribed can have a positive impact on people; however, some medication can be used inappropriately by people who do not have the prescription. How do you plan to store your medication securely?

- It is imperative that medication is taken as prescribed to maintain an accurate therapeutic level. What would the impact be if you stopped taking your medication as prescribed?

- What experience do you have with managing your own prescription (calling for a refill, going to the pharmacy, checking for accuracy)?

LESSON 2: DAILY HABITS

DISCUSSION POINTS

Throughout school, people may have been around to help remind you of the things you will need during your school day. Perhaps your parents woke you up for school and gave you your medicine, a friend may have reminded you to turn in your homework, or a teacher may have told you when you need to ask for more money for your lunch account. When you come to college, you will be responsible for managing all of these things independently. Having a system in place for being prepared for your day can have a positive impact on your experience at college.

GUIDING QUESTIONS

- What support have you had in the past to remember everything you will need for your day?

- What systems have you set up to manage your day independently?

- What types of things might you need for your classes each day?

- What things will you need every day other than class supplies?

- Previously, if you lost something, it would have been easy to go to your parents for assistance. At college, you can do that as well, but it is more effective to know who can help you on campus. Who would you call if you lost your room key? Identification card? Meal card? Debit/credit card?

LESSON 3: SELF-CARE

DISCUSSION POINTS

Growing up, you may have heard your parents tell you to take a shower, or brush your teeth every day, but why is this important? When you come to college, you will be surrounded by new people in classes and your residence hall. They all will be meeting you and each other for the first time. It is possible that you may not place the same importance on hygiene as neurotypical people, but in this new environment, it is very important to remind yourself to always be clean. Taking care of your basic needs each day will help you maintain your physical and emotional health. By creating a schedule for these self-care tasks, you will develop a habit and may no longer need to be reminded by the adults in your life.

GUIDING QUESTIONS

- What types of activities are included in what is referred to as self-care?

- How many hours of sleep do you need to be rested and at your optimal level of functioning during the day?

- What types of things can distract you from getting an appropriate amount of sleep?

- How would getting less sleep than you need affect you during the day?

- College campuses have dining facilities and meal plans set up for students to use daily, but students with ASD sometimes struggle in these environments. Dining halls can be loud and may not have food choices that meet your preferences. How can you manage this while still taking care of your nutritional health?

- Getting the appropriate amount of physical exercise daily will also help you take care of yourself. What kind of physical activity do you enjoy?

- What is your level of independence with hygiene tasks?

- What system have you set up to remind yourself to take showers, brush your teeth, wash your hair, wash your face, clean your clothes, etc.?

- You will be attending classes, studying, and possibly living with other people when you come to college. It is important to recognize that the choices you make have an impact on those around you. How do you plan to keep your backpack, study space, and living space clean and organized?

LESSON 4: KNOW YOUR RESOURCES

DISCUSSION POINTS

College professionals know that students come to campus with a variety of strengths and opportunities for growth. Knowing your own strengths and areas that will need support will set you up for the best chance of success. As a full-time student, you should plan to spend no less than 40 hours per week on your studies. That can create a tremendous amount of anxiety for some students, but there are resources available on campus to support any need a student may have.

GUIDING QUESTIONS

- What type of support have you had previously in school?

- If you get sick when you are at college, where would you go to get help?

- What are your areas of academic weakness in which you may need support?

- If you are having a difficult time with something, do you know where to go for assistance?

- What things do you think you may need support with on campus?

CHAPTER 5: COMMUNICATION IN PERSONAL LIFE

LESSON 1: ACTIVE COMMUNICATION

DISCUSSION POINTS

As students come to college, the level of social interaction will be amplified. As a student with ASD, you will need to pay very close attention to the changes in the social requirements and develop a new strategy for managing the various rules of social interaction in college. A large portion of the message in any social contact is passed through body language and verbal cues. As you learn these cues, it may be a good idea to document how facial expressions may impact the message being sent by you or others. Recognizing the message people are sending through their body language is another skill that you can practice to help better manage the art of conversation. The skill of maintaining appropriate conversations is something that you will need to practice. Knowing how to enter a conversation, sharing the conversation, gauging your reactions, and knowing when the conversation is over may not come naturally to you, but it is something that you can master with some practice.

GUIDING QUESTIONS

- How well do you maintain eye contact?

- How can you initiate conversations with new people?

- What are you doing to practice your social skills?

- What are some verbal cues that someone is not interested in conversation?

- What are some non-verbal cues that you can recognize?

- How aware are you of your reactions to others (your non-verbal body language)?

- Do you pay attention to the personal space of others?

LESSON 2: SHARING THE CONVERSATION

DISCUSSION POINTS

One of the things that make people with ASD unique is the vast knowledge about specific topic areas. While this knowledge is admirable and often contributes to career goals, this topic area can often monopolize conversation. It is very important that you recognize the interest level of people in the conversation. Perhaps you should observe conversations prior to joining to assess whether you have anything related that you can contribute. Pay close attention to the age level of those with whom you are communicating. For instance, if you are talking with a group of high school students about college, it would not be appropriate to share with them all the knowledge you may have about weapons. Conversely, if you are talking with a group of other college students over lunch, it would not be seen as age appropriate to share all the information you know about "My Little Pony" or cartoons. Finally, it is essential that you know the "no-go" topics of conversation on a college campus. While you may know a great deal of information about certain areas, talking about this information is not always appropriate. It is advisable to avoid talking about your knowledge of weaponry, killing, or bombs with people who don't know you very well. These topics could be interpreted as threatening or fear-inducing and could get you into trouble with campus police, Judicial Affairs, or worse. If these are your topics of interest, you should only communicate openly about this information with people who know you very well.

GUIDING QUESTIONS

- How do you make a conversation mutual (shared)?

- In what situations would your conversations be more formal? Less formal?

- How do you make communication styles different between a friend and a professor?

- How often do you talk about your interest areas?

- Current events are good topics of conversations. What are some current events you are comfortable discussing?

- What are some verbal cues that someone else is trying to end a conversation?

- Are you easily distracted in a conversation?

- How do you end conversations?

- In a group of people, how are you at acknowledging others?

- What things can you do to practice starting, engaging in, and ending a conversation appropriately?

LESSON 3: PERSONAL SPACE AND TONE OF VOICE

DISCUSSION POINTS

Something that often makes people uncomfortable is standing too close during a conversation. This is called invading people's personal space. The distance you can maintain in a conversation is dependent on a couple of things: the relationship status with the other person and the activity going on around you. This identifying information will also help you regulate your volume and the tone of voice you should use in the conversation. These skills are difficult; however, as with anything, analyzing people's reactions and shifting your approach will help you through this process.

GUIDING QUESTIONS

- How aware are you of your personal space?

- How aware are you of the personal space needs of others?

- Are you able to adjust the volume of your voice or do you need prompts to do so?

- Do you consider your environment in determining your tone and volume of voice?

- How do you communicate your frustrations, and when is it appropriate?

- What are some non-verbal cues that indicate you are too close to someone?

- Are you aware of how others interpret your tone and how congruent that is to your intentions/motive?

- What would be an appropriate distance between you and a professor when having a conversation about grades?

- Are you aware of how you process information in conversation? How do you communicate that?

CHAPTER 6: STRESS MANAGEMENT
LESSON 1: SYMPTOMS OF STRESS

DISCUSSION POINTS

Any life transition can be difficult to manage. This is particularly so if you are moving onto a college campus for the first time, have not established a routine yet, and don't have your typical support system around you to help you manage the stress. The first step in learning to manage stress on your own is to know what stress feels like for you. There are many physical indicators that signify that you are beginning to feel anxious, and if you learn these signs, you will be able to gain control of the stress in your life more quickly. The physical symptoms of stress are different for every person, but the signs could be something as simple as feeling tension in the muscles in your neck and shoulders or could be chest pain and shortness of breath. Although chest pain can be a sign of anxiety, if you are feeling chest pain of any kind, you should get it evaluated by a medical professional immediately.

People with ASD tend to have a much lower stress tolerance. This may make the transition to college a challenge because this new environment is filled with sensory experience: many people talking, different smells, fluorescent lights flashing, fire alarms, new food options, etc. These new experiences can combine to create stress and anxiety if you are not aware of your stress triggers or hot spots. These triggers vary greatly for everyone. A trigger can be a change in routine for one person and a fire alarm for the next. Knowing what can trigger anxiety for you can help you control your stress before it escalates beyond your control.

GUIDING QUESTIONS

- What does stress feel like in your body?

- What level of stress have you experienced before?

- When stress approaches a full anxiety attack, what might it feel like?

- What type of digestive issues have you experienced during times of stress?

- What type of sleep pattern disruption have you experienced as a result of stress?

- What situations can cause stress for you?

- If you had a change in routine, how anxious would that make you?

- If your professor changed class location, how much stress would that cause for you?

- If you did not get enough sleep, how much stress would you experience?

LESSON 2: STRESS CAN LEAD TO ANGER: CONTROLLING YOUR EMOTIONAL RESPONSE

DISCUSSION POINTS

The everyday stressors in your life could easily build upon each other to create a difficult situation to manage. In the college environment, regardless of diagnosis or difficulty, you will be held accountable to the same student code of conduct as any other student, so it will be vital that you are able to recognize your stress indicator, triggers, and know how to cool yourself before you reach a situation where you have an angry outburst. Regardless of your intention or the cause of an outburst, as a student, you will be held accountable for your behaviors. To be responsible for this, you can establish a visual model to help you and others understand what level of stress/anxiety you are experiencing. If you imagine a scale from 1 to 5 with 1 being everyday, manageable stressors and 5 being the level of stress that may lead to an outburst, you can help yourself avoid unnecessary judicial or legal ramifications.

Another side of anxiety is what we term meltdowns. While meltdowns often appear to be temper tantrums, these true meltdowns are much more. As a person with ASD, you may know your limit of sensory exposure. If you reach a point beyond your limit, you may feel a meltdown coming on. A meltdown can be cathartic for you as your brain triggers you to expel unnecessary information and stimuli, but it can be scary and threatening to people who do not understand this. It is important to develop a plan or a place to go and person to see if you approach this level of anxiety. Knowing your safe place/safe person can make this process more manageable.

GUIDING QUESTIONS

- What types of situations would cause you to reach a level higher than 3 on a scales of 1 to 5?

- What strategies can you use to reduce your stress level at this stage?

- What is your established plan to help you manage the stressors of college life?

- Who can be your person who will support you in the event of a meltdown?

- What are some things that could happen if you do not appropriately control stress and it reaches the anger stage?

- What could happen if you ever reached a level 5 on your stress/anxiety scale?

LESSON 3: COPING STRATEGIES TO REDUCE STRESS

DISCUSSION POINTS

As you develop a better understanding of your stress indicators, triggers, levels of stress/anxiety, and cooling methods, you will become more adept at controlling the impact of your stress throughout the process. Many people use exercise as a method to reduce their level of stress while others opt for spending time outside in the sunshine and fresh air. Academic stress is one area you can control by being a responsible college student. If you approach your classes in a planned way and avoid procrastinating, your level of stress around your academic requirements will be greatly reduced. The more prepared you are for class discussions, homework, and exams, the better you will feel about your progress. This academic success will help alleviate academic stress with few other methods needed.

There are a few specific methods of stress reduction that are known to be helpful for people with ASD. Isolated muscle control, deep breathing techniques, and guided visualization all take into account the detailed nature in which many people with ASD operate. In these methods, people are assisted in focusing on specific muscles or breathing patterns, or they are guided through specific visualization activities to help them reach a point of calm. Staying open to any option of stress release can help you become a master of your own stress management plan.

GUIDING QUESTIONS

- What coping strategies have worked for you in the past?

- How have you depended on others to help you manage your anxiety?

- What has been your experience with guided visualization?

- What coping strategy are you willing to explore further?

LESSON 4: KNOW YOUR RESOURCES

DISCUSSION POINTS

Any college campus will have a plethora of resources available to all students to access in a time of need. Knowing who or what these resources are and where they are located before you need them will make the process much more manageable in the event of an anxiety attack or meltdown. As with anything, the more planning you put into place before you experience a need for support, the better off you will be. Take some time to identify the resources on your campus with physical locations and phone numbers.

GUIDING QUESTIONS

- What are some of the resources available on your campus to help you in times of stress?

- Where is the college Counseling Center located on your campus?

- What situations may arise that would cause you to depend on the Dean of Students Office?

- What situations may cause you to need to reach out to a peer or friend on campus as the first point of contact?

- When might a situation elevate so much that your family members should be contacted?

CHAPTER 7: PERSONAL RESPONSIBILITY IN ACADEMICS
LESSON 1: ATTENDANCE

DISCUSSION POINTS

Responding to new independence when they arrive on a college campus challenges college students. One important change to note is the responsibility students have to go to class. As simple and obvious as it may seem, attending college courses can be difficult for many students, when there is not a clear attendance policy that demands students attend. The general consensus on a college campus is that attending class is a personal responsibility for students and those who value their academic endeavors should take attendance as a personal rule rather than a classroom rule. It is surprisingly easy to find a reason not to attend a class at 8 o'clock on Monday morning when it's raining outside and no homework is due. To respond to this challenge, students with ASD should create an attendance policy of their own standard when one is not provided for them, in order to establish a sense of structure concerning attendance. There is another responsibility for students when they do miss a class for a warranted reason. Professors will not seek out the student to provide missed material, so the student needs to use professional email communication techniques to inquire about missed material or to explain an absence. Students can also recognize the classroom community and seek missed material from a classmate before consulting with the professor.

GUIDING QUESTIONS

- What is the attendance policy for each of the classes in which you are enrolled?

- What are some ways you can create consistency with class attendance?

- Explain the process you would go through if you felt sick and needed to miss a class.

- What steps will you take in your living environment to ensure you make it to each class?

- How can you use technology to ensure you do not forget about a class time?

- What are some reasons you might need to miss class?

- How can you know if your professor excuses a missed class?

- Why is it necessary to track your attendance in class?

LESSON 2: OUT-OF-CLASS ASSIGNMENTS

DISCUSSION POINTS

While students certainly spend some time in the classroom in order to learn an academic subject, a certain number of out-of-class assignments will reinforce the material students are exposed to in class. College coursework is not optional. Even readings from a textbook to prepare for in-class discussion are not optional. If an assignment is listed on the syllabus or discussed in class, consider it essential to passing the course. Student mastery of course information is the goal for professors when they assign out-of-class work. Students need to develop an organized plan for working on assignments in order to complete them, and ensure they are turned in to the instructor by the assignment deadline. It may take some time for students with ASD to become efficient at using time wisely when it comes to assignments, but a general rule is to allow more time to complete an assignment than you think is necessary. In addition, students should ask for clarification of an assignment that is confusing because "I didn't understand the assignment" is not a valid excuse for not turning it in when you're in college.

DISCUSSION QUESTIONS

- What is the most difficult aspect of completing assignments for you?

- How can you improve your management of time to make sure all your assignments are completed by their deadlines?

- What kinds of clarifying questions might you need to ask a professor about an assignment that is confusing to you? Where else can you seek clarification?

- How would you go about prioritizing out-of-class assignments for different classes?

- What kind of assignments do you struggle with the most—papers or essays, reading long chapters, solving math problems, constructing a project, preparing for a presentation?

- Brainstorm some ways to remind yourself about assignment deadlines.

LESSON 3: GROUP WORK

DISCUSSION POINTS

More often than not, college courses include some sort of group work component. Some classes may require a group presentation or project worth a significant portion of a student's grade, while others may simply encourage spontaneous group discussions in class as part of a general participation grade. For students with ASD, group work can be a daunting and dreadful task. Not only are students with ASD challenged by mastering the academic content of the group work like their neurotypical peers, but they also need to consider social skills and strategies for interacting in groups that may not come naturally to them. The increased pressure to perform socially as well as academically can be difficult, but some basic social rules can make a difference in the outcome of the group work for students with ASD. First, understanding that most students, with and without ASD, struggle with group work can be a relieving thought for someone who dreads group work. The initial meeting with a group is often the most difficult as social niceties are exchanged. Students can prepare by rehearsing an introduction before meeting their groups. Working in a group using one's strengths is a great way to ensure a successful group experience, but this requires that students are familiar with and comfortable sharing their strengths. Being aware that different people have different opinions, values, and personalities is one way students can prepare mentally for working in groups. There is no way to avoid group work in college. However, each group will be different and the process becomes easier with a little practice.

GUIDING QUESTIONS

- How does group work impact you as a student with ASD?

- What talents and skills do you bring to groups?

- How can you use the characteristics of ASD that you might demonstrate to your advantage when working with groups?

- Describe the kind of greeting you will offer when meeting with a group for the first time.

- What can you do to ensure that the work is evenly distributed between members of the group?

LESSON 4: STUDY HABITS

DISCUSSION POINTS

Understanding the need to develop study skills that are effective for a student's learning style is essential to making the most out of studying and preparing for assignments and exams in college. Students will need to manage time effectively, set realistic study goals, monitor effort, and develop frequent study plans. While support will be available for students on the spectrum at their respective campuses, students need to take responsibility for their study habits. Knowing how much and when to study is important as students take on the different assignments and exams that are scheduled during any given week. Using a watch, clock, or device with reminders can help students monitor their study time. Setting goals and establishing a series of mini-tasks that will lead to completion of a larger task is another habit worth practicing. Of course, students need to consider all the ways in which their study habits are influenced by external stimuli, and then prepare a solution to these influences. For example, if you know that noise is a distraction for you when studying, then studying in the library is better than trying to study in a coffee shop. Recognizing these personal preferences when studying makes a difference in the implementation of study skills and the development of strong study habits.

GUIDING QUESTIONS

- What is your favorite place to study?
- How can you monitor time spent on assignments?
- Who can you ask to help you create a study plan?
- What materials will you need to study for each class?
- Why do you think it is important to take breaks while studying?
- How can you find motivation for studying?

LESSON 5: MAJOR/WORK/CAREER

DISCUSSION POINTS

Students in college will eventually transition into some post-college work environment. Preparing for this while they are still in college is essential for making sure they are prepared and ready for this transition. The first step is choosing an academic major that will prepare students for a career that fits their skills and interests. There are resources on campus that are available to help students make this decision. This can be a stressful decision early in the college experience, but once it is made, students have the opportunity to pursue a goal with intent and purpose as it matches their interests and passions. Sometimes academic majors do not lead to a career in the same field, but this is how experience influences interests while students are engaged on a college campus.

Studying a subject that is interesting is still a worthwhile endeavor, even if this does not result in a related career. Meeting with faculty and advisors to determine the best course of action once students have committed to an academic major keeps them on track and prepares them for graduation. Exploring career opportunities and gaining insight about the career options available to students in relation to their academic interests is another way students can engage with campus. The college years are a great time to take advantage of job shadowing, internships, part-time jobs, and networking events in preparation for the post-college work environment, while also allowing students to practice social skills and decide if the experience is something they would like to pursue professionally.

GUIDING QUESTIONS

- What is your academic major? If you have not yet decided, what are some majors that interest you?

- How can you use campus resources to help identify which major is right for you?

- In what ways does your major apply to your future career goals?

- What is a good way to be mindful of the balance between academic, social, and career-related activities throughout college?

- What are your strengths as a student? How can these be applied to a future job?

- What do you consider to be areas for improvement for you as a student? How can you improve in your weaker areas to be a better potential employee?

CHAPTER 8: CAMPUS SOCIAL LIFE
LESSON 1: THE CAMPUS SOCIAL STRUCTURE

DISCUSSION POINTS

A college campus is one arena in which there is a community of people who share a common interest—higher education. Just by attending a university, students are a part of this community. Students with ASD can use the support of campus administration and support staff to ensure that their involvement as part of the campus community is positive. Connecting with people on a college campus might be a challenge when students do not know anyone very well before attending. Students with ASD might have a particularly difficult time adjusting to the abundance of social activities and events on campus during the transition stage. The key to feeling like part of the community is to intentionally invest your social engagement in part of the community in which you have an interest. For example, if you are interested in outdoor recreation, spend your time and effort adjusting to a social activity or group that is structured around this interest instead of feeling like you need to attend all events and be part of many different groups in order to be part of the community. You are already part of the larger campus community and a smaller sense of community that is more likely to facilitate and foster new relationships and opportunities for practicing social skills is an aspect of college life that many students find rewarding.

GUIDING QUESTIONS

- How does your campus create a sense of community?

- What level of involvement within the campus community can you realistically commit to when taking into consideration your academic schedule, personal life, wellness, and interests?

- Who can you work with on your campus to receive some more information about certain campus groups?

- What type of campus club would you be interested in starting if there is not one already established?

LESSON 2: LEARNING OPPORTUNITIES

DISCUSSION POINTS

College is much more than academic coursework, and students can benefit from taking part in their campus' social atmosphere. Students with ASD in particular can use structured campus social activities to practice new social skills and build relationships with peers who share common interests. Students can pursue academic activities in a social context through major-focused clubs or groups, leadership development opportunities, social clubs, service-oriented groups, and interest-driven clubs. Most college campuses feature study abroad options, career services and programs, and an array of student organizations. Taking advantage of all of these learning opportunities makes sense for students on the spectrum as they foster social skills in a safe environment that is all available due to the tuition and fees students pay to attend the college.

All college students need to take advantage of their learning opportunities in order to increase their marketability as potential employees. Involvement on a college campus is often an essential component of a student's application and resume sought by those employers who value employees who have applicable experience beyond the classroom. For students with ASD, seeking out opportunities to increase their marketability can induce some anxiety, but taking part in structured and interest-driven campus activities and organizations can prepare students for similar social interaction in the workplace.

- What are a few learning opportunities on your campus that you would be interested in pursuing?

- Where can you locate information about these learning opportunities?

- Is there a type of group or student organization that you feel would be a welcome addition to your campus' social environment?

- What social skills should you remember when attending social activities or events on your campus?

- What does it mean to be "marketable"?

- How marketable are you as a potential employee currently?

- What college clubs, groups, or activities would be related to your academic pursuits in college?

- Brainstorm some ways to improve your marketability during your first year in college.

- How can you build on these improvements during the following years as you prepare for graduation?

LESSON 3: BALANCING IT ALL

DISCUSSION POINTS

While the campus social life at many colleges is a fun and exciting element of the college experience for students, a balance must be maintained in order to be successful. Academic demands increase from high school to college, and the basic academic workload is often much more intense than it was in high school. Even general education courses taken by students early in their college careers are often characterized by writing assignments, lab projects, and less frequent exams with a higher volume of knowledge and context. Students are encouraged to take advantage of the social opportunities as they adjust to the campus way of life, but are cautioned against prioritizing social life over academic work. Likewise, students should integrate some degree of social interaction into their lives in order to practice skills needed for campus and community interaction and to take a break from all the studying. Just as neurotypical students cannot realistically manage entire weeks of non-stop studying or entire weeks of being constantly engaged socially, students with ASD need to establish a system of time management that balances their involvement with academic and social demands. A basic guideline for developing a structure for balance is to use prioritizing strategies to isolate tasks and events that are given more importance for students. For example, one such standard strategy students use is to accomplish an academic task before any social activity. Students with ASD will benefit from a consistent and organized planning system to ensure balance.

GUIDING QUESTIONS

- What personal interests are especially important to you?

- Describe your ideal balance between social and academic life.

- Explain the social and academic demands you experience daily as a college student, and give your personal reasoning for the need to keep things balanced.

- What are some consequences of a lack of balance at college?

- Brainstorm some planning options that will prevent an imbalance between your social life and your academic life. Which of these would you be most likely to adhere to consistently?

CHAPTER 9: RELATIONSHIPS

LESSON 1: DEFINING RELATIONSHIPS

DISCUSSION POINTS

College students who are on the autism spectrum are challenged with understanding ambiguous social rules in order to develop and maintain healthy relationships. In order to use practiced social skills in an effective way to build a relationship, one must have a solid understanding of six general categories of relationships. Knowing when another subject in a relationship is a stranger, an acquaintance, a friend, someone a student is dating, a boyfriend or girlfriend, or a life partner can be understood best when these general categories have definitions that offer some guidance for an otherwise fluid and unpredictable concept of relationships.

GUIDING QUESTIONS

- Describe a relationship that was particularly difficult for you to define.

- What kinds of signals can you look for to understand your relationship with someone?

- Give an example of someone who is your acquaintance.

- What are some general tips for managing safe online relationships and interactions?

LESSON 2: RECOGNIZING RELATIONSHIP LEVELS

DISCUSSION POINTS

College students who have an understanding of relationships are able to navigate their social life with intentional interactions structured by some knowledge of relational boundaries and the implications regarding personal relationships. In order to successfully transition between relationship levels, you can rely on knowledge about varying levels of relationship progression to determine the most appropriate ways to interact with the people in your life. Although there is not a scientific formula for navigating social interactions and understanding relationships, following a general guide like the relationship level algorithm (see page 173) creates an opportunity for students to utilize a certain degree of structure when establishing relationships on the college campus.

GUIDING QUESTIONS

- Explain the order of the relationship level progression pathway as it is described in the text.

- What are some appropriate actions that are involved in each level of the progression? (For example, waving or smiling politely at someone with whom you have had a class when you pass them at a local grocery store is an appropriate action for acquaintances.)

- What is the difference between dating someone and having a boyfriend or girlfriend? What actions might be involved in each level that are different from the other?

- What kinds of relationships are difficult to place into a relationship level or category?

- Share an example of a time when you were confused about a relationship and where it would have been in terms of the relationship level progression pathway.

LESSON 3: SEXUALITY AND GENDER IDENTITY

DISCUSSION POINTS

The college environment often creates opportunities for students to explore their sexuality and gender identity. There are several concepts related to the development and understanding of sexuality and gender identity, including some complex terms and the notion of social construction, but the most important thing college students with ASD need to remember regarding sexuality and gender identity is that there are resources available on campus to help sort through these issues. Students on the spectrum can learn that social construction of sexuality and gender influences societal perceptions that are often apparent through the way many students interact with the college environment. College students should be prepared to recognize these social norms in terms of sexuality and gender identity, but also be aware of resources available on the college campus to provide support for those students who may find that their sexuality or gender identity is outside of the stereotypical and socially constructed categories, or those students who seek to further their knowledge of these subjects.

GUIDING QUESTIONS

- What kind of campus resources could you seek if you have questions about sexuality and gender identity?

- What other elements of your culture are socially constructed?

- How does having ASD as a college student impact the way you perceive sexuality and gender identity?

LESSON 4: NON-OPTIONAL SOCIAL COMPLIANCE

DISCUSSION POINTS

Some social rules can be ambiguous, but there are a few social rules that require an explanation of their Non-optional Social Compliance to demonstrate the necessity to adhere to a standard social code. Even if students do not personally understand these social rules, they must be followed on a college campus. Understand that the perception of those individuals students interact with on a college campus is the pivotal element to these social rules regarding relationships. It does not matter if a student's intentions were just, as a lack of understanding of social rules is not an excuse when someone perceives behavior to be threatening, harassing, or stalking.

GUIDING QUESTIONS

- Give one example of an action that could be perceived as threatening.

- What behavior could replace that threatening action in order to adhere to rules of Non-optional Social Compliance?

- Give one example of an action that could be perceived as harassing.

- What behavior could replace that harassing action in order to adhere to rules of Non-optional Social Compliance?

- Give one example of an action that could be perceived as stalking,

- What behavior could replace that stalking action in order to adhere to rules of Non-optional Social Compliance?

BIBLIOGRAPHY

Attwood, T. (1998) *Asperger's Syndrome: A Guide for Parents and Professionals.* London, UK: Jessica Kingsley Publishers.

Attwood, T. (2006) *The Complete Guide to Asperger's Syndrome.* London, UK: Jessica Kingsley Publishers.

Baron-Cohen, S. (2003) *The Essential Difference: Men, Women and the Extreme Male Brain.* London, UK: Penguin.

Baron-Cohen, S., Leslie, A.M., and Frith, U. (1985) "Does the autistic child have a theory of mind?" *Cognition 21,* 37–46.

Buron, K.D. (2007). *A 5 is against the law! Social boundaries: Straight up! An honest guide for teens and young adults.* Shawnee Mission, KS: Autism Asperger Publishing Company.

Buron, K.D., Brown, J.T., Curtis, M., and King, L. (2012) *Social Behavior and Self-Management: A 5-Point Scale for Adolescents and Adults.* Shawnee Mission, KS: AAPC Publishing.

Carley, M.J. (2008) *Asperger's from the Inside Out.* New York, NY: The Penguin Group.

Dubin, N. (2009) *Asperger Syndrome and Anxiety: A Guide to Successful Stress Management.* London, UK: Jessica Kingsley Publishers.

Freedman, S. (2010) *Developing College Skills in Students with Autism and Asperger's Syndrome.* London, UK: Jessica Kingsley Publishers.

Frith, U. (2003) *Autism: Explaining the Enigma (Second Edition).* Oxford, UK: Blackwell.

Frith, U. and Hill, E. (2003) *Autism: Mind and Brain.* Oxford, UK: The Royal Society.

Grandin, T. (2011) *The Way I See It: A Personal Look at Autism and Asperger's.* Arlington, TX: Future Horizons, Inc.

Grandin, T. and Baron, S. (2005) *The Unwritten Rules of Social Relationships: Decoding Social Mysteries through the Unique Perspectives of Autism.* Arlington, TX: Future Horizons, Inc.

Harpur, J., Lawlor, M., and Fitzgerald, M. (2004) *Succeeding in College with Asperger Syndrome: A Student Guide.* London, UK: Jessica Kinglsey Publishers.

Hendrickx, S. (2008) *Love, Sex and Long-Term Relationships: What People with Asperger's Syndrome Really Really Want.* London, UK: Jessica Kingsley Publishers.

Kasal, J.P. (2013) *Guided imagery and visualization.* Available at www.support-for-add-and-autism-spectrum.com/Guided_imagery.html, accessed on May 24, 2013.

Lawson, W. (2003) *Build Your Own Life: A Self-Help Guide for Individuals with Asperger's Syndrome.* London, UK: Jessica Kingsley Publishers.

Lawson, W. (2005) *Sex, Sexuality and the Autism Spectrum.* London, UK: Jessica Kingsley Publishers.

Lawson, W. (2006) *Friendships the Aspie Way.* London, UK: Jessica Kingsley Publishers.

Ozonoff, S., Dawson, G., and McPartland, J. (2002) *A Parent's Guide to Asperger Syndrome and High-Functioning Autism: How to Meet the Challenges and Help Your Child Thrive.* New York, NY: The Guilford Press.

Palmer, A. (2006) *Realizing the College Dream with Autism or Asperger Syndrome: A Parent's Guide to Student Success.* London, UK: Jessica Kingsley Publishers.

Patrick, N.J. (2008) *Social Skills for Teenagers and Adults with Asperger Syndrome: A Practical Guide to Day-to-Day Life.* London, UK: Jessica Kingsley Publishers.

Wolf, L.E., Brown, J.T., and Bork, G.R.K. (2009) *Students with Asperger Syndrome: A Guide for College Personnel.* Shawnee Mission, KS: Autism Asperger Publishing Company.

INDEX

A Freshman Survival Guide for College Students with Autism Spectrum Disorders

The Stuff Nobody Tells You About!

Haley Moss

Foreword by Susan J. Moreno

Paperback: £14.99 / $19.95

ISBN: 978 1 84905 984 8

160 pages

MUST HAVE!

How do you know which college is right for you? What happens if you don't get on with your roommate? And what on earth is the Greek system all about? As a university student with High-Functioning Autism, Haley Moss offers essential tips and advice in this insider's guide to surviving the Freshman year of college.

Chatty, honest and full of really useful information, Haley's first-hand account of the college experience covers everything students with Autism Spectrum Disorders need to know. She talks through getting ready for college, dorm life and living away from parents, what to expect from classes, professors and exams, and how to cope in new social situations and make friends.

This book is a must-read for all students on the autism spectrum who are about to begin their first year of college, parents and teachers who are helping them prepare, and college faculty and staff.

• • • • • • • • • • • • • • • • • • • •

Contents: Acknowledgments. Foreword by Susan J. Moreno. Introduction. 1. While You're Still in High School. 2. Getting Ready for College. 3. Dorm Life 101. 4. Academics. 5. Professional Development – Career Prep, Involvement, and More! 6. Social Life and Social Issues. 7. Stress and Mental Health. 8. Living Independently. 9. Home and Growing Up. Helpful Websites.

• • • • • • • • • • • • • • • • • • • •

HALEY MOSS is a 19-year-old student with High-Functioning Autism. She has recently completed her Freshman year at University of Florida where she is pursuing a Bachelor of Science in Psychology and a Bachelor of Arts in Criminology. She is also taking a minor in Disabilities in Society. Haley is the author of Middle School: The Stuff Nobody Tells You About, she is a keen advocate for autism, and she is a frequent speaker at autism events. She has won numerous awards including a Hope for Children "Teen Hero Award" and she was named one of the University of Florida's "Gators of Tomorrow - Top 25 Freshman Leaders". She is also a talented artist. Website: http://www.haleymossart.com/myART/Welcome.html Facebook: www.facebook.com/HaleyMossART Twitter: https://twitter.com/haleymossart.

JUN 1 5 2015

Date Due
